Math INNOVATIONS **COURSE 2**

MOVING MATH FORWARD THROUGH CRITICAL THINKING AND EXPLORATION

Sizing Up Solids

Focusing on Angles, Surface Area and Volume

Suzanne H. Chapin

M. Katherine Gavin

Linda Jensen Sheffield

Kendall Hunt
publishing company

ACKNOWLEDGMENTS

Math Innovations Writing Team

Authors

Suzanne H. Chapin

M. Katherine Gavin

Linda Jensen Sheffield

Project Manager

Janice M. Vuolo

Teacher Edition Team

Jennifer M. MacPherson

Ann Marie Spinelli

Alice J. Gabbard

Writing Assistants

Jacob J. Whitmore

Kathy Dorkin

Jane Paulin

Mary Elizabeth Matthews

Mathematics Editor

Kathleen G. Snook

Assessment Specialist

Nancy Anderson

Advisory Board

Jerry P. Becker

Janet Beissinger

Diane J. Briars

Ann Lawrence

Ira J. Papick

Unless otherwise noted, photos in this book and on the cover used under license by ShutterStock, Inc.

Kendall Hunt
publishing company

www.kendallhunt.com

Send all inquiries to:

4050 Westmark Drive

Dubuque, IA 52004-1840

1-800-542-6657

Production Date: 2015

Printed by: LSI

United States of America

Batch number: 431242

Printed in the United States of America

1 2 3 4 5 6 7 8 9 10 16 15 14 13

Sizing Up Solids:
Focusing on Angles, Surface Area and Volume
Table of Contents

UNIT GOALS

STUDENT EDITION

Sizing Up Solids: Focusing on Angles, Surface Area and Volume

After studying this unit, you should be able to:

- Classify solids and analyze vertices, edges and faces of polyhedrons.

- Represent three-dimensional prisms and pyramids using two-dimensional nets.

- Construct two-dimensional shapes such as triangles and draw orthogonal and isometric representations of solids;

- Explore cross sections of solids;

- Develop an understanding of points, lines (including parallel and perpendicular lines) and rays;

- Develop the concept of angle measure, including the use of protractors and goniometers;

- Solve problems involving complementary, supplementary, and vertical angles as well as the sum of angle measurements in a triangle;

- Understand the formulas for area and circumference of circles and use them to solve problems;

- Explore formula for the surface area of prisms and pyramids and use them to solve problems;

- Determine the volume of solids such as cubes, triangular prisms, rectangular prisms and composite figures.

Dear Student Mathematician,

We live in a three-dimensional world. We see and use solid figures such as prisms every day. But we also work with geometric drawings in two-dimensions. For example, we draw designs using circles and other shapes for logos. Sneakers are packaged in rectangular boxes.

Have you ever had to make sure you had enough wrapping paper to wrap a present? Or wondered how much stuff would fit into a backpack? Have you had to figure out how to measure an angle or make a circle of a particular size for a game board? You will be able to answer these questions and more by the end of this unit.

In this unit, *Sizing Up Solids: Focusing on Angles, Surface Area and Volume*, you'll be introduced to a student-run company, *Containers for Kids*, that manufactures containers and boxes in different shapes. To learn about the work of *Containers for Kids*, you will analyze and classify three-dimensional figures and learn how to draw them using three different methods. You will explore the measurement of angles and angle relationships formed by intersecting lines. You'll learn about nets of shapes and explore how they can be folded into solids. Similarly, you will learn how boxes can be taken apart to form nets. You'll also be introduced to surface area, which is the amount of area needed to cover or wrap a solid. When you are painting a room or determining the amount of cardboard needed for a box, you are calculating surface area. Finally, you will investigate how to find the volume of some common solids, such as rectangular and triangular prisms, and how volume is affected when you make a miniature version of a prism. Determining the amount of space in a box is a practical application of volume.

We hope you enjoy learning about surface area and volume and the world of solid geometry.

Mathematically Yours,
The Authors

Suzanne H. Chapin   *M. Katherine Gavin*   *Linda Sheffield*

Spatial Visualization

We live in a three-dimensional world. Every object has dimensions that are described with terms such as *length*, *width*, *height*, *depth*, *breadth* and *thickness*. We often study characteristics of 3-D shapes, or space figures, by examining pictures and drawings. Visualizing a solid figure based on a drawing in a textbook is essential to understanding geometry. Furthermore, understanding how two-dimensional drawings and three-dimensional shapes are related is an important part of understanding geometric concepts.

LESSON 1.1 Characteristics of Three-Dimensional Shapes

 **Start It Off**

1. Draw and label three polygons and three non-polygons.

2. Name ten different polygons. Name four shapes that are not polygons.

3. Write a mathematical definition of the term *polygon*.

Polyhedrons

Our daily lives would be much more complicated if we didn't have containers. Imagine carrying your books, school supplies and lunch to school without a backpack! Containers are three-dimensional figures that come in all shapes and sizes and can be classified in a number of ways.

Some containers can be classified as polyhedrons.

Polyhedrons   **Not polyhedrons**

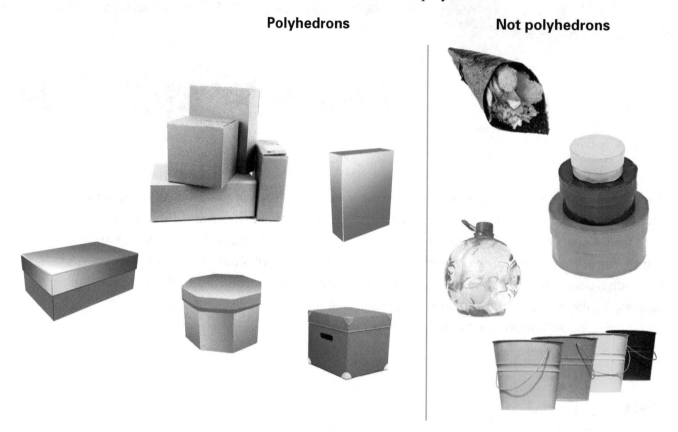

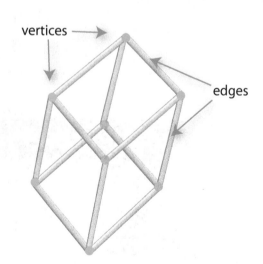

1. Examine the drawings and list some of the characteristics of polyhedrons.

Polyhedrons are three-dimensional shapes with no curved surfaces. The flat surfaces are called faces. Each face is in the shape of a polygon. An edge of a polyhedron is a line segment where two faces meet. A vertex of a polyhedron is a point where three or more edges meet.

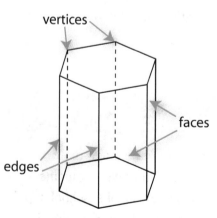

Building Prisms

Some polyhedrons are prisms. Building prisms can help you learn their features.

All prisms have two identical, parallel faces. These faces are called the bases of the prism.

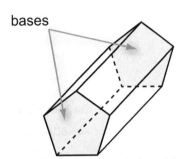

bases

The bases are connected by faces that are parallelograms. The faces that are NOT bases are called lateral surfaces. In the prism below, the lateral surfaces are all rectangles.

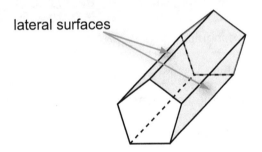

lateral surfaces

Prisms are named by the shape of their bases. The prism above is a pentagonal prism. Prisms can be positioned in any direction. That is, they do not have to "sit" on their bases.

A cube is a special type of rectangular prism in which all of the faces are squares.

2. To help you learn about prisms, build these models using construction materials. In these models, toothpicks represent the edges and marshmallows represent the vertices. Name each type of prism.

a)

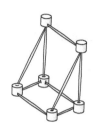

b)

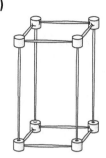

c)

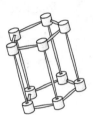

d)

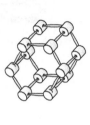

e)

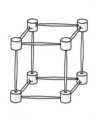

3. Explain why each of the models that you built can be classified as a prism. Identify the bases and lateral surfaces on each prism.

4. Find the number of faces, vertices and edges for the prisms. Remember to count each base as a face. Try to determine these numbers first by visualizing the prisms. Then, use your models to check your answers. Put this information into a table.

Name of Prism	Faces	Vertices	Edges
Triangular prism			
Cube			
Rectangular prism			
Pentagonal prism			
Hexagonal prism			
Octagonal prism			

5. **a)** What patterns do you notice in the table?

   b) Write rules for finding the number of faces, the number of vertices and the number of edges for a prism with an n-sided base.

   c) Explain why your answers to Part b make sense.

Building Other Polyhedrons

6. Build a model that is **not** a prism of:

   a) a polyhedron with six edges

   b) a polyhedron with six faces

   c) a polyhedron with five vertices

   d) Explain how you created the model for Part b.

MATHEMATICALLY SPEAKING

▶ pyramid
▶ tetrahedron
▶ apex

What types of models did you make for Question 6? Were they pyramids? A pyramid is a polyhedron that has a single base and triangles for its other faces. These triangular faces are the lateral surfaces of the pyramid. A pyramid is named by the shape of its base. The pyramids in Egypt are square pyramids. A tetrahedron is a special triangular pyramid that has equilateral triangles for its base and its lateral surfaces.

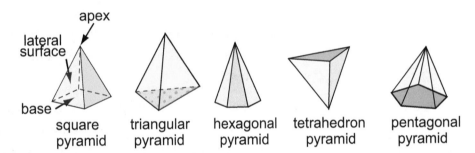

apex

lateral surface

base

square pyramid   triangular pyramid   hexagonal pyramid   tetrahedron pyramid   pentagonal pyramid

The vertex opposite the base of a pyramid is called the apex.

7. Examine the models and drawings of pyramids. Fill in the table with the number of faces, vertices and edges. Remember to count each base as a face.

Name of Pyramid	Faces	Vertices	Edges
Triangular pyramid			
Square pyramid			
Pentagonal pyramid			
Hexagonal pyramid			

8. Write rules for finding the number of faces, the number of vertices, and the number of edges for a pyramid with an *n*-sided base. Explain why your rules make sense.

Cross Sections

MATHEMATICALLY SPEAKING

▶ cross section
▶ plane

So far you have examined the number of faces, edges and vertices of some common polyhedron. Next you will investigate cross sections of prisms and pyramids. A cross section is the region formed by the intersection of a solid and a plane. Cross sections are two-dimensional shapes that are obtained when solids are sliced by a plane.

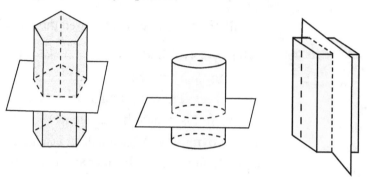

What is a plane? A plane is flat and goes on forever in all directions. You can imagine a plane by thinking of a thin sheet of paper that cuts through a solid.

9. Make a cube using toothpicks and mini-marshmallows, or use a hollow, plastic cube and fill it with colored water. Using either of these models, experiment to see which of the following shapes you can make by slicing the open cube with an index card to represent a plane or by tilting the colored water in the plastic cube to represent a plane. Before investigating a new cross section, make sure your model is still in the shape of a cube or realign the water in the plastic cube to be level. Record with a picture or a description how you produced the shape. Not all are possible!

   a) square

   b) rectangle

   c) triangle

   d) hexagon

   e) circle

   f) parallelogram

The drawings below show cross sections of a pyramid with a square base. The green plane intersects the pyramid in different locations and produces different cross sections, shown in red.

a)

b)

c)

10. Describe how the plane slices the square pyramid in Parts a–c. Use the terms, 'parallel' and 'perpendicular,' if appropriate.

11. What is the shape of each cross section?

12. Imagine repeatedly slicing the trapezoidal prism below so that each of the slices is the same size and shape. How might you do this?

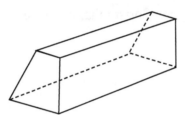

Wrap It Up

What is a cross section? What types of cross sections can be formed when a prism or pyramid is sliced by a plane?

MATHEMATICALLY SPEAKING

▶ apex

▶ base

▶ cross section

▶ cube

▶ edge

▶ face

▶ lateral surface

▶ plane

▶ polyhedron

▶ prism

▶ pyramid

▶ tetrahedron

▶ vertex (vertices)

MATERIALS LIST

▶ Optional:
toothpicks and
mini-marshmallows

 **Write
About It**

1. Triangular prisms can have bases that are equilateral, isosceles or scalene triangles. Do these triangular prisms have the same numbers of faces, vertices and edges? Why or why not? Use pictures to illustrate your points.

2. List five common objects that are examples of prisms or pyramids. Indicate the type of prism or pyramid each object represents.

3. Visualize a prism with 10-sided bases (called a decagonal prism). Explain how you can determine the numbers of faces, vertices and edges on this prism.

4. Name a type of prism that has exactly:

   a) 5 faces.

   b) 12 edges.

   c) 6 vertices.

   d) Make up a similar question about a type of prism. Solve it.

5. I'm a prism with 24 vertices. How many faces do I have? How many edges? What type of prism am I?

6. Every August at the Sunapee Fair, artists build tent frames out of tree saplings or rigid plastic tubing in the shape of open prisms and pyramids. The edges are connected at the vertices using rope or duct tape.

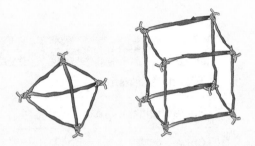

a) How many feet of tubing would an artist need to build the frame of a cube that is 5'9" tall?

b) The artist also plans to build a tetrahedron using the same amount of tubing she is using for the cube. How long will each of the tetrahedron's edges be? Explain your reasoning.

7. Name a type of pyramid that has exactly:

a) 5 faces.

b) 12 edges.

c) 6 vertices.

8. Think about the numbers of edges found on different prisms. Why are these numbers always multiples of 3? You may want to use a drawing or model in your explanation.

9. a) A prism has 12 vertices. How many faces does it have? How many edges does it have? What type of prism is this?

b) A pyramid has 20 edges. How many faces and vertices does it have? What is its name?

10. Leonhard Euler, a Swiss mathematician (1707–1783), discovered a relationship between the numbers of faces, vertices and edges of polyhedrons. Copy and fill in the table below.

Name of Polyhedron	Faces	Vertices	Edges
Triangular prism			
Rectangular prism			
Cube			
Pentagonal prism			
Hexagonal prism			
Square pyramid			
Triangular pyramid			
Hexagonal pyramid			

a) Use the patterns in the table to write a rule to show how the numbers of faces, vertices and edges are related. Use F, V and E as your variables. This rule is called Euler's Formula.

b) Use algebra to show why Euler's Formula is true for prisms. In Question 5 in the lesson, you wrote rules for the number of vertices, the number of faces, and the number of edges in a prism. Substitute these rules for V, F and E in the equation, $V + F - E = 2$ and simplify.

c) Find another interesting fact about Leonhard Euler.

11. In the past, the Camp-On Tent Company manufactured tents shaped like half cylinders. Now their tents are shaped like triangular prisms. Why might the Camp-On Tent Company have changed their tent design?

12. Imagine slicing the following two prisms. First, identify the type of prism. Then explain how to repeatedly slice each prism so that all the slices are congruent.

a) 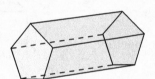 **b)**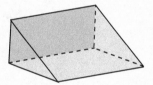

13. Charlie made a 5-story tower out of blocks. His sister came along and knocked it all down, except for the base layer. The base is a cross section of the tower. What did the tower look like before it was knocked down?

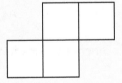

14. Imagine or build a rectangular prism with square bases.

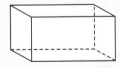

  a) How might you slice it to get a cross section in the shape of a rectangle?

  b) How might you slice it to get a cross section in the shape of a triangle?

  c) How might you slice it to get a cross section in the shape of a square?

15. Write definitions for the terms "cross section" and "plane."

16. Using the cube below, give the name of the polygon that describes the cross section that cuts through the following points. Points M, N, P, Q, and R are midpoints of edges.

    a) through E, A, C and G

    b) through P, M, R and Q

    c) through E, G and B

Think Beyond

Identify the points a plane would intersect the cube in order to make the following cross sections.

    d) a trapezoid

    e) a hexagon

    f) isosceles triangle

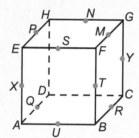

Think Back

17. Identify the place value of the 7.

    a) 62,046.9750

    b) 839.8997

18. Round the numbers in Questions 17a and 17b to the nearest tenths place.

19. What is the difference between a prime number and a composite number? Give four examples of each type of number.

20. Estimate each answer. Then, find the exact answer. Show your work.

    a) $61.040 - 5.99 =$

    b) $-7.812 + 49.05 =$

21. Two-thirds of an apple pie was left over from dinner Tuesday night. Maria decided to have a piece of the pie as a snack after school Wednesday. She had a piece that was $\frac{1}{4}$ of what had been left over. How much of the whole pie did she have?

LESSON 1.2 Nets

➡️ Start It Off

MATHEMATICALLY SPEAKING

▸ dimension

The size of a solid object is measured in three dimensions. Dimensions tell us how tall, how wide, and how long the object is.

1. What are some of the words used to indicate the dimensions of a container or solid?

2. The height of a prism is always the vertical distance. The longer of the remaining sides is the length of the prism. Indicate the length, width and height of each prism.

a)

3 cm
7.1 cm
4.5 cm

b)

4.5 cm
7.1 cm
3 cm

c)

7.1 cm
4.5 cm
3 cm

d)

4.5 cm
4.5 cm
4.5 cm

3. What is the name of the prism where the three dimensions have the same value? Which prism is this?

4. Since all faces of a rectangular prism are rectangles, different pairs of faces can be named as the bases. What are the dimensions of all possible bases in the prisms in Question 2?

Nets of Cubes

Do you or your family have music CDs? Now that so much music is available as MP3s, many people do not listen to their CDs as often. But they don't want to discard their CDs since they may use them to download songs onto other electronic devices.

Heather and Maria, two friends, have decided to make and decorate boxes to store their CDs.

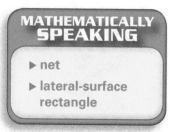
They found that one way to construct a box is to make a net and then fold it up. A **net** is a two-dimensional pattern that can be folded into a three-dimensional shape.

Heather and Maria think a cube might be a good shape for a box to hold their CDs.

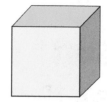

Below is a net of a cube. The net consists of six squares since there are six square faces on a cube. Visualize yourself folding the long rectangular portion, made up of four squares, to start forming your cube. These four squares together are called the lateral-surface rectangle—a rectangle formed by the lateral surfaces of a prism.

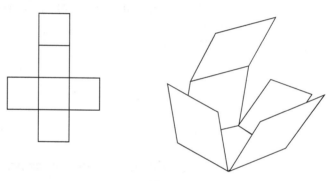

Now fold up the two remaining squares to form the bases of the cube.

1. For each net, identify the lateral-surface rectangle. Explain how to fold the net into a cube.

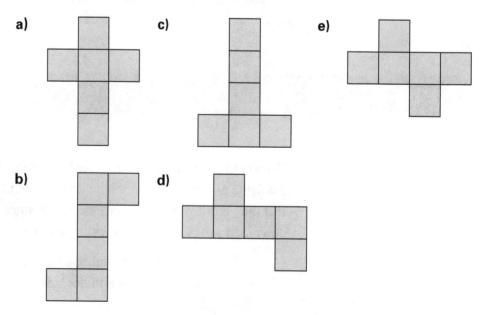

a)

c)

e)

b)

d)

2. How are all of the nets in Question 1 the same? How are they different?

Maria and Heather measured some CD cases before making their cube-shaped boxes.

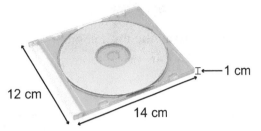

3. a) What are the dimensions of the smallest cube that can hold CD cases?

b) Sketch and label a drawing of the net of this CD box. What are the dimensions of its lateral-surface rectangle? What are the dimensions of its bases?

c) How many CD cases can be stored in this cubic box?

Nets of Rectangular Prisms

Another possibility is to store the CD cases in a box that is a rectangular prism, but is not a cube. However, before you consider rectangular-prism boxes, examine the net of a CD case.

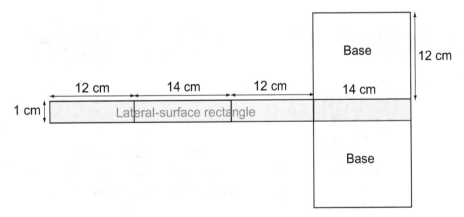

4. a) Explain how to fold up the net of the CD case above into a rectangular prism.

b) What are the dimensions of the bases? What are the dimensions of the lateral-surface rectangle?

c) Draw a different net that also can be folded into a CD case with these dimensions.

5. **a)** Give the dimensions of a rectangular prism-shaped box that will hold exactly 5 CD cases and another that will hold exactly 12 CD cases.

b) Draw the net of either box in Question 5a. Label all the dimensions.

Examine this net on centimeter graph paper and this prism. Do both the net and the prism represent the same box?

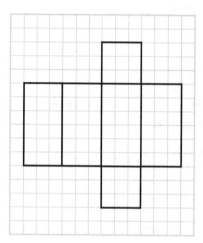
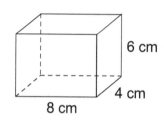

6 cm
4 cm
8 cm

6. When the net on the left is folded, what are the dimensions of the resulting prism? Can you use it to store CDs? Why or why not?

7. Examine the prism on the right. Decide which faces will be the bases, and then imagine unwrapping the lateral-surface rectangle. What are the dimensions of the lateral-surface rectangle and the bases? You may want to make a sketch of the net.

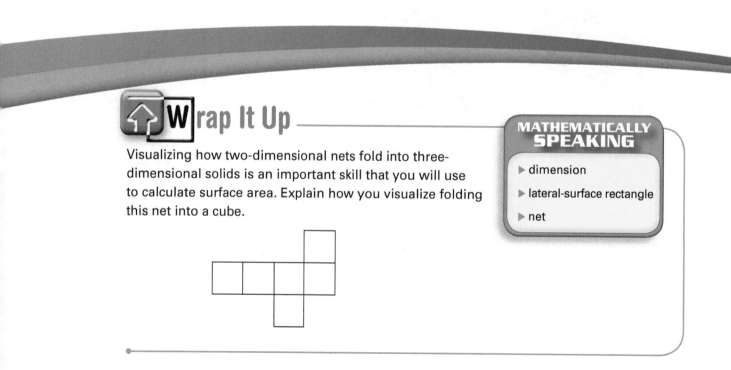

⬆W rap It Up

Visualizing how two-dimensional nets fold into three-dimensional solids is an important skill that you will use to calculate surface area. Explain how you visualize folding this net into a cube.

MATHEMATICALLY SPEAKING

▶ dimension

▶ lateral-surface rectangle

▶ net

MATERIALS LIST

► Oaktag or cardboard (optional) for ring box
► Graph paper

Write About It

1. Find a small rectangular prism. Measure its dimensions in millimeters. Decide which of the faces will be the bases. Make a sketch of the net of the prism.

2. Predict whether or not these nets fold into cubes. Then sketch the nets on grid paper and cut them out to check your answers.

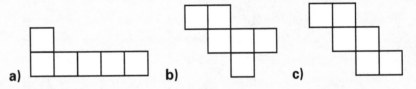

a) b) c)

3. Copy the nets and fill in the blank faces so that opposite faces on the folded cube would be labeled with the same letters.

a)

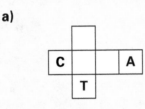

b)

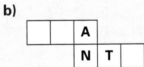

c)

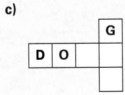

4. A cube used in a particular board game has an edge length of $2\frac{1}{4}$ inches. The cube is missing, so Juan decides to make a paper cube to replace it. How much paper will he need to make a net of this cube?

5. Is it possible to cut the net of the cube in Question 4 out of a regular sheet of notebook paper? Explain.

6. Some boxes do not have tops. Predict which of the nets below can be folded into a cube-shaped box with an open top.

a)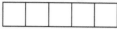

g)

b)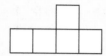

h)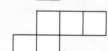

c)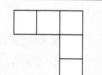

i)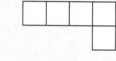

d)

j)

e)

k)

f)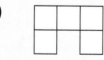

l)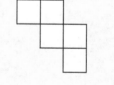

7. On grid paper, draw the nets in Question 6 that fold into cube-shaped boxes with an open top. Place an X on the face that is opposite the open top when folded.

8. What are the dimensions of a box you would make to hold CD cases? How many CDs could fit in your box?

9. In your own words, explain the mathematical meaning of the term *net*. Use it in a sentence.

10. Rings are often packaged in small cube-shaped boxes. Create a net for a box that could be used to hold a ring for your finger. Decorate the net and fold it into a box. What are the dimensions of your ring box?

11. Is a cube a polyhedron? Why or why not? Is a cube a prism? Explain.

12. On a number cube, the faces opposite each other always sum to 7.

a) What number is on the face opposite the 4? Opposite the 5? Opposite the 1?

b) Draw these nets below. Place the digits from 1 to 6 on each net so it could be used as a number cube. Check by folding.

i) 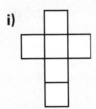　　　ii) 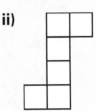　　　iii)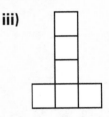

Think Beyond

13. Find all possible nets of a cube. Explain how you know that you have found all of them.

Think Back

14. Determine the measure of each angle. Use a protractor.

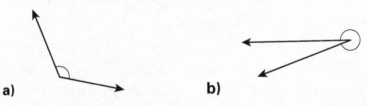

a)　　　　　　　　　　　　　b)

15. Gretta said that the absolute value of an integer is equal to the opposite of that integer. Is she right or wrong? Explain.

16. Place these fractions in order from least to greatest without finding their common denominator: $\frac{8}{5}, \frac{8}{3}, \frac{8}{7}$.

17. Write a word problem that can be solved using the division problem $37 \div 4$. Solve your problem.

18. Lyle wrote that $\frac{13}{12} > \frac{7}{6}$ since twelfths are greater than sixths. Do you agree or disagree with Lyle? Explain.

Three-Dimensional Drawings

➡ Start It Off

1. On graph paper draw four different parallelograms, each with a base of 4 centimeters and an area of 8 square centimeters. Describe how they are different.

2. How do you identify the base and the height of a parallelogram?

3. Find the area of the following parallelograms.

a)

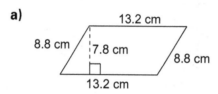

13.2 cm
8.8 cm
7.8 cm
8.8 cm
13.2 cm

b)

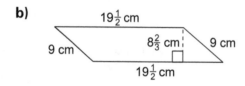

$19\frac{1}{2}$ cm
$8\frac{2}{3}$ cm
9 cm
9 cm
$19\frac{1}{2}$ cm

c)

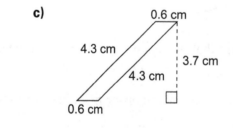

0.6 cm
4.3 cm
3.7 cm
4.3 cm
0.6 cm

Three-Dimensional Drawings

Have you ever tried to draw a pyramid or prism? It's a bit tricky! How did you make your drawing look realistic? In this lesson, you will investigate a number of ways to make drawings of three-dimensional shapes.

Follow these directions:

Example 1

Step 1 Draw a base of a rectangular prism. This is the surface of the figure that will face you and should be drawn in the normal manner.

Step 2 For a prism, draw the second base so that corresponding sides are parallel, as shown below.

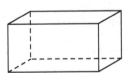

Step 3 Connect the vertices using a ruler. Use solid lines for visible edges and dashed lines for hidden edges.

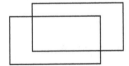

Example 2

Step 1 Draw a base of a square pyramid. This is the surface of the figure that will face you and should be drawn in the normal manner.

Step 2 For a pyramid, mark a point diagonally to the left or right of the base for the apex.

Step 3 Connect the vertices using a ruler. Use solid lines for visible edges and dashed lines for hidden edges.

You can lightly shade some of the faces to make them look solid.

 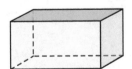 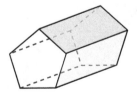

Notice that the surfaces facing you are drawn as you would see them (squares, rectangle and a pentagon).

1. Make your own drawings of some prisms and pyramids. Have some show only visible edges, and have others show hidden faces, vertices and edges. Label a lateral surface, a base, a vertex and an edge on one of your drawings. Label the apex on one pyramid.

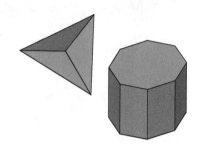

   Write the name of the type of shape beneath each drawing.

2. a) Make a 3-D drawing of a cube using the method above.

   b) Draw a cube using the following method: draw a regular hexagon and inside the hexagon, draw three lines as shown. How do the images of the cube in Parts a and b differ?

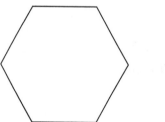 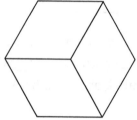

   c) Sometimes pyramids are drawn with one vertex facing forward. Draw these pyramids. Explain your method.

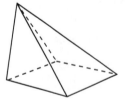 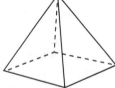

Isometric Drawings

MATHEMATICALLY SPEAKING

▶ isometric dot paper
▶ isometric drawing
▶ perspective

Another way to make 3-D drawings is to use special paper called isometric dot paper. On isometric dot paper, the dots are arranged in a triangular pattern. Drawings on this paper are called isometric drawings. You can connect the dots on isometric dot paper to form shapes. Isometric drawings are used in drafting, video game design and pixel art. Isometric drawings do not show perspective—that is, portions of objects do not appear smaller or larger to indicate their distance from the viewer—but objects do look three-dimensional! In isometric drawings, figures are oriented on the page so that you are looking straight at an edge rather than a face of the solid.

3. Here is an isometric drawing of a cube.

   a) How many faces are visible?

   b) How many edges are visible?

   c) Draw a cube on isometric dot paper.

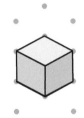

4. Examine these isometric drawings of structures made with four cubes. Which isometric drawings are of the same structure? Which drawing includes a hidden cube?

A.

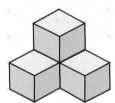

C.

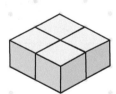

B.

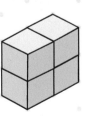

D.

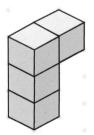

5. a) Draw the structures in Question 3 on isometric dot paper. First, draw vertical segments and then connect them to form cubes.

b) Make other four-cube structures by connecting four cubes in various ways. Then make isometric drawings of your structures.

c) Pick one structure and draw it to show a different orientation.

6. Draw all possible four-cube structures. How do you know you have them all?

Draw and rotate four-cube structures using NCTM's Isometric Drawing Tool at: http://illuminations.nctm.org/ActivityDetail.aspx?ID=125.

 **W rap It Up**

What hints can you give other students for making 3-D drawings using both methods?

MATHEMATICALLY SPEAKING

▸ isometric dot paper

▸ isometric drawing

▸ perspective

MATERIALS LIST

▶ Isometric dot paper, centimeter or inch cubes

On Your Own

 Write About It

1. One of your classmates was absent and missed the lesson on three-dimensional drawing. Write detailed directions for drawing a prism and a pyramid.

2. Draw a shape with two bases that are parallel but not congruent. Label all features of the shape. Is your shape a prism? Why or why not?

3. Use isometric dot paper and draw all structures that can be made with exactly three cubes. How many different structures are possible?

4. Which of these drawings represent congruent structures?

? **Hint**
See page 156

A.

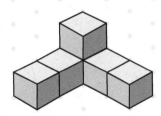

C.

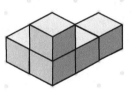

B.

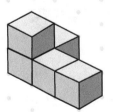

D.

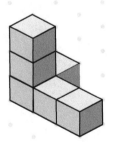

5. Describe how you determined which structures in Question 4 are congruent.

6. Make an isometric drawing of a futuristic city.

7. Examine the drawings below.

   a) How many cubes does it appear were used to build each structure?

   b) Sometimes the cubes used to build a structure are hidden from view in an isometric drawing. If two cubes must share at least one face, which of these structures could have hidden cubes? Explain.

   i)

   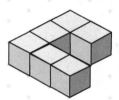

   iii)

   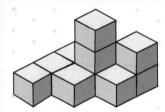

   ii)

   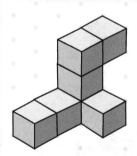

   iv)

   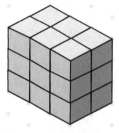

8. Make a drawing of a large cube constructed from 64 unit cubes. What are the dimensions of the cube?

Think Beyond

9. **a)** Pentominoes are two-dimensional figures made with five squares. You can also build three-dimensional structures using five cubes. At least one face of every cube must touch at least one face of another cube. Build five-cube structures and then draw each structure on isometric dot paper.

   b) Explain how you approached the problem of building all five-cube structures.

10. Evaluate $|y^3 - y|$ when $y = {}^-3$.

    A. ${}^-24$

    B. ${}^-30$

    C. 24

    D. 30

11. What type of polygon makes up the lateral faces of a prism in the shape of a shoebox? How many edges and vertices does this prism have?

12. Solve.

    a) $\frac{x}{9} = 112$

    b) ${}^-9w = {}^-3$

13. Kyle has a short-cut for finding a product when one factor is a power of 10. He simply attaches zeroes based on the power of 10 (one zero for 10^1, two zeroes for 10^2, three zeroes for 10^3, and so on) to the other factor. Create one multiplication problem where Kyle's short-cut works. Create another multiplication problem where Kyle's short-cut does not work. Revise Kyle's rule.

14. What does it mean to say that the chances of winning a game are 50-50?

Three Different Views

→ Start It Off

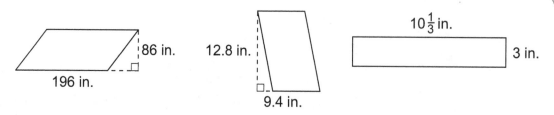

1. Sketch the parallelograms above. For each, draw a diagonal line connecting two opposite vertices to create two triangles. Determine the areas of the triangles formed.

2. How is the formula area of each triangle related to the area of the parallelogram?

3. How might you use this relationship to help you remember the formula for the area of a triangle?

Orthogonal Drawings

Drawings by architects and engineers present different 2-D views of a 3-D structure. These drawings show how the structure would look when viewed from the right, left, front, back, bottom or top.

MATHEMATICALLY SPEAKING

▶ orthogonal drawing

The six drawings on the right below are views of the prism on the left. They are called orthogonal drawings. What do you notice?

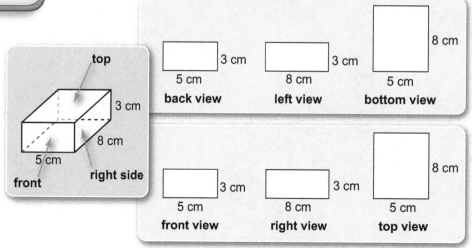

You can draw orthogonal views of cube structures.

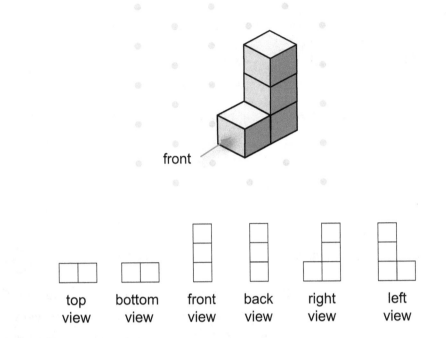

In many structures, opposite views are mirror images. In such cases, you can describe the structure using just the top, front and one of the side views.

1. Draw and label sketches of the orthogonal views of these prisms. Label the dimensions on these views. If two views are mirror images, you only need to draw one of them.

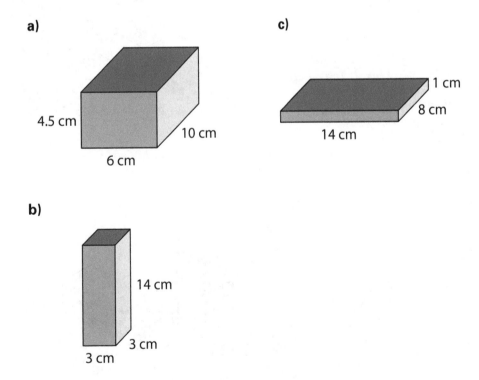

2. Use these orthogonal views to sketch a three-dimensional drawing of the following prisms. Include the dimensions in your drawings.

a)

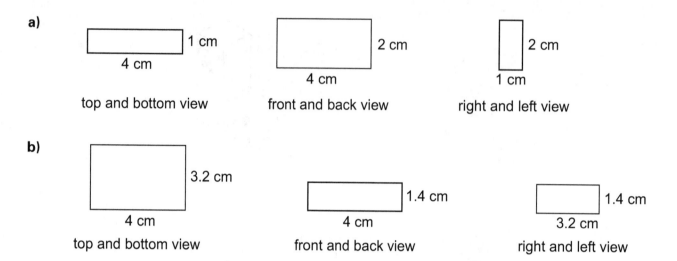

1 cm
4 cm
top and bottom view

2 cm
4 cm
front and back view

2 cm
1 cm
right and left view

b)

3.2 cm
4 cm
top and bottom view

1.4 cm
4 cm
front and back view

1.4 cm
3.2 cm
right and left view

3. Build the following structures using cubes. Then, using graph paper, draw the views of each structure. If two views are mirror images, you need to draw only one of them. Label the views.

a)

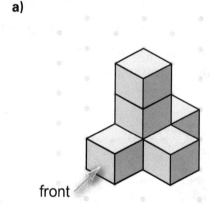

front

b)

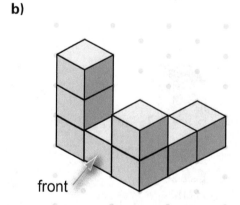

front

4. For each set of views, build the structure. You can assume that opposite views are mirror images. In some cases, there is more than one possible structure.

a)

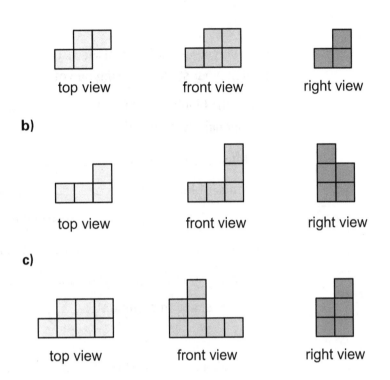

top view   front view   right view

b)

top view   front view   right view

c)

top view   front view   right view

rap It Up

You have built three-dimensional cube structures based on two types of two-dimensional drawings— isometric drawings and orthogonal drawings. Which type of two-dimensional drawing do you think is easier to translate into a three-dimensional structure? Why? What are the advantages and disadvantages of each type of drawing?

MATHEMATICALLY SPEAKING

▶ orthogonal drawing

MATERIALS LIST

▶ Ruler, centimeter or inch cubes (optional)

Write About It

1. How do you use orthogonal views of a structure to visualize the structure? Explain your strategies using one of the buildings from this lesson.

2. Fill in the blanks. Use: polyhedrons, depth, isometric, prisms, orthogonal, pyramids, three.

   Architects regularly create _____ and _____
   1   2
   drawings of buildings. For _____ drawings they draw at
   3
   least _____ views of the structure. These drawings do
   4
   not show _____. Architects also create three-dimensional
   5
   renderings of buildings called _____ drawings. Many buildings
   6
   are in the shape of common _____ such as _____
   7   8
   and _____.
   9

3. **a)** Heather and Maria (from Lesson 1.2) decided to make orthogonal drawings of their CD boxes. Sketch and label the top, front and side views of their boxes if each is 16 cm long, 14 cm wide, and 20 cm high.

   b) What would the three views look like if each box was 16 cm by 16 cm by 16 cm?

4. Match the isometric and orthogonal drawings.

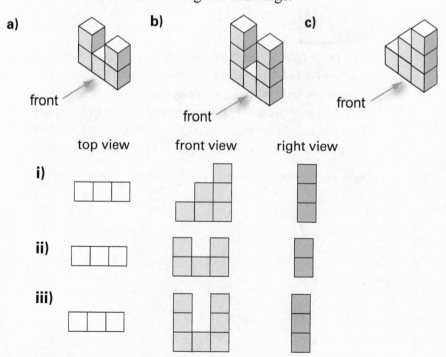

5. a) Draw a prism for which all the orthogonal views are identical.

b) Draw a prism for which there are only two different orthogonal views.

6. Is it possible to make this building from non-interlocking cubes? Why or why not?

7. Examine the following isometric drawing. Label each orthogonal view as front, right, left, top, back or not possible.

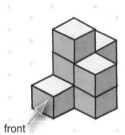

front

a)

d)

b)

e)

c)

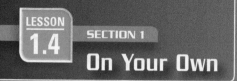
8. Sketch the orthogonal views of these structures.

a)

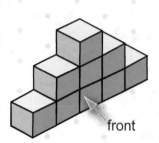

front

b)

front

9. Draw orthogonal views for the prism.

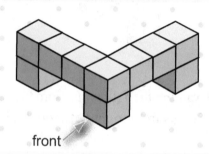

3 cm

8 cm

15 cm

front

Think Beyond

10. What is the minimum number of cubes that can be used to build a structure with these views? Demonstrate your answer using unit cubes.

top view

front view

right view

Think Beyond

11. Does the orthogonal drawing below represent a unique three-dimensional structure? Why or why not?

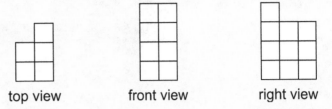

top view   front view   right view

Think Beyond

12. Build this structure. Make a 3-D drawing of this structure. How might you use the top view to record the number of blocks used to build the structure?

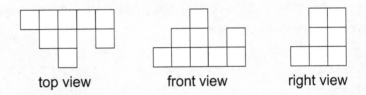

top view   front view   right view

Think Back

13. Represent each situation with an integer.

   a) a withdrawal of $53

   b) Badwater Basin of Death Valley is 282 feet below sea level.

   c) a drop of 5°

   d) Zeke gained 12 yards in the football game.

14. $\frac{5}{6} \cdot -\frac{6}{10} \cdot -\frac{3}{7} =$

15. Frank can rent an unlimited number of DVDs for $14.99 each month. The DVDs arrive by mail. Frank then pays $0.52 to mail each DVD back. Last month he received eight DVDs, watched them, and then returned them. On average, how much did Frank spend for each DVD last month?

16. Explain your strategy for simplifying the fraction $\frac{63}{108}$ to lowest terms.

17. Find the perimeter of the trapezoid by measuring it to the nearest tenth of a centimeter.

Optional Technology Lesson for this section available in your eBook

Sum It Up

Characteristics of Solids

- Polyhedrons are three-dimensional shapes whose faces are polygons. There are many types of polyhedrons, such as rectangular prisms, triangular prisms, octagonal prisms, cubes, pyramids and tetrahedrons.

  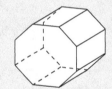

- Polyhedrons have faces, edges and vertices. The vertex opposite the base of a pyramid is called the apex.

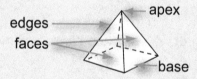

- Prisms are one type of polyhedron. Prisms have two identical faces that are parallel. These faces are called the bases. The other faces are called lateral surfaces. Lateral surfaces of prisms are parallelograms.

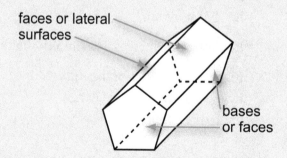

- In a prism with an *n*-sided polygon as the base, the number of faces is $n + 2$, the number of vertices is $2n$ and the number of edges is $3n$.

> **Example**
>
> **Pentagonal prism**
>
> The base of a pentagonal prism has 5 sides.
> The prism has 7 faces ($5 + 2 = 7$).
> The prism has 10 vertices ($2 \cdot 5 = 10$).
> The prism has 15 edges ($3 \cdot 5 = 15$).

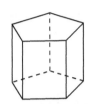

- A cross section is a two-dimensional shape that is obtained when a solid is sliced by a plane. Many different two-dimensional shapes can be formed when intersected by a plane.

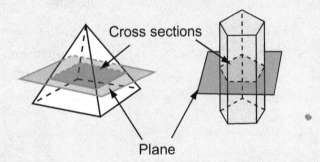

Nets

- A net is a two-dimensional pattern that can be cut out and folded to make a three-dimensional shape.

- There are many nets that fold into a cube. To fold the net below, visualize folding the lateral-surface rectangle first, and then folding the side faces in to close the solid.

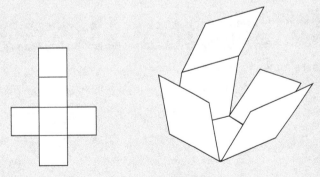

- The dimensions of a prism can be identified in its net.

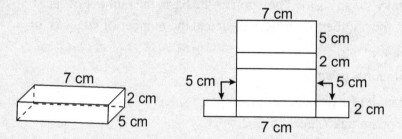

Drawing 3-D Shapes

- A space figure can be represented in a variety of ways—with an isometric drawing, with orthogonal drawings, or with a simple 3-D drawing.

- It is important to be able to represent and interpret space figures on paper. Your ability to visualize three-dimensional objects and their two-dimensional views will improve with practice!

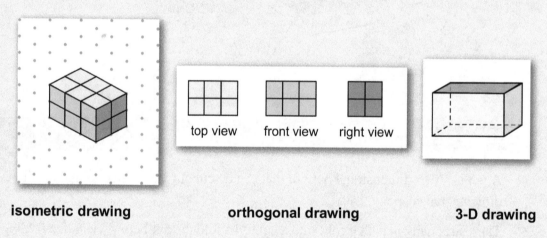

isometric drawing   **orthogonal drawing**   **3-D drawing**

MATHEMATICALLY SPEAKING

Do you know what these mathematical terms mean?

▶ apex	▶ isometric dot paper	▶ plane
▶ base	▶ isometric drawing	▶ polyhedron
▶ cube	▶ lateral surface	▶ prism
▶ cross section	▶ lateral-surface rectangle	▶ pyramid
▶ dimension	▶ net	▶ tetrahedron
▶ edge	▶ orthogonal drawings	▶ vertex (vertices)
▶ face	▶ perspective	

Study Guide

Part 1. What did you learn?

1. A rectangular prism is 4 in. by 2 in. by 1 in.

    a. Describe five characteristics of this prism.

    b. Make a 3-D drawing and show a cross section of the prism.

    c. Sketch a net of the prism.

    d. Make an isometric drawing of the prism.

    e. Draw the orthogonal views of the prism.

2. Explain the differences and similarities between an apex and a vertex.

3. Given the top, front and right views, draw the figure below on isometric dot paper.

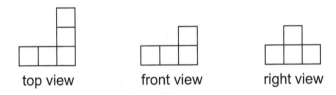

| top view | front view | right view |

4. Is this a polyhedron? Why or why not?

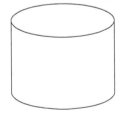

5. **a.** How many edges does a pyramid with a base of 29 sides have?

    b. How many edges does a 29-gonal prism have?

    c. Explain how to use visualization to determine the number of edges in pyramids and prisms.

    d. A horizontal plane slices through a pyramid with a base of 29 sides. The plane slices the pyramid about half way up. What would the cross section look like?

6. What kind of a prism has six identical faces?

7. The figure on the right below is a rotation of the figure on the left. Label the dimensions of the figure on the right.

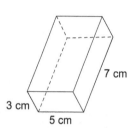 

8. Explain how you know how many faces a prism has if the base polygon has *n* sides.

9. Define these terms using words and drawings.

    a. tetrahedron

    b. polygon

    c. lateral-surface rectangle

    d. prism

    e. base

    f. plane

Part 2. What went wrong?

10. Robbie's teacher asked him to draw and label the front, right and top views of the rectangular prism below.

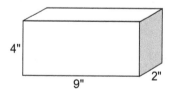

Robbie knows how to draw and label the front and the right views but he is confused about how to draw and label the top since he doesn't see measurements for the top face. What would you do or say to help Robbie draw and label the top view?

What's Your Angle?

Throughout history, people have used signs and symbols to describe the world around them. Mathematicians around the world share a common language of symbols. In this section, you will learn some of the symbols and notation systems that are part of the language of geometry. In particular, you will learn about angle measurement and the relationships among angles in shapes such as triangles.

LESSON 2.1 Points, Lines and Rays

Start It Off

Refer to the number line below.

1. At what letter are each of the following located?

   0.54 _____

   $\frac{9}{8}$ _____

   30% _____

   $\frac{13}{16}$ _____

2. Where would you put point *I* to indicate 22%?

3. Describe three strategies you would suggest to a classmate for placing fractions, decimals and percents on a number line.

In ancient Greece, a mathematician named Euclid was interested in expanding upon the most basic ideas in geometry. He wrote a set of 13 books called *Euclid's Elements* that discussed very elementary ideas. For nearly 2,000 years, every "educated" person was expected to be familiar with ideas presented in these books.

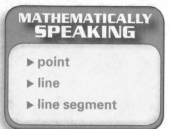

MATHEMATICALLY SPEAKING

▶ point
▶ line
▶ line segment

One of the most basic ideas in *Euclid's Elements* is that of a point. A point is considered to be a location in space that has no dimensions (size) or orientation (direction). That means that it has no length, width, height or thickness. A point is often represented by a dot, • and named by an upper case letter, such as *A*.

A line is a set of points that form a straight path extending infinitely in two directions. A line is named by any two points it passes through. The line pictured below can be called "line *AB*," which is denoted $\overleftrightarrow{AB}$.

If we connect two points, such as *A* and *B*, then we form a line segment, which is the portion of the line between those two points, including the endpoints.

A line segment has one dimension, length, but has no width or height. A line segment has two endpoints, such as *A* and *B*. The line segment with endpoints *A* and *B* is called "segment *AB*" and is denoted $\overline{AB}$. We use linear measures such as feet, inches, centimeters and meters to measure line segments.

MATHEMATICALLY SPEAKING

▶ ray
▶ collinear

A ray is a part of a line that starts at one point on that line and extends forever in one direction. Think about how this relates to a ray of sunshine that starts at the sun and extends (almost) infinitely in one direction.

A ray is named by its starting point and any other point it passes through. For example, the ray pictured above is called "ray *AB*," which is denoted $\overrightarrow{AB}$.

Two points are enough to determine a unique ray, line or line segment. Three or more points that lie on the same line are called collinear points.

Using these simple ideas about points, lines, rays and line segments, we can describe many of the ideas that make up the study of geometry.

1. How is the mathematical concept of a ray, which starts at a single point and extends infinitely in one direction, similar to a model such as the drawing of a ray? How is it different?

Use the diagram below for Questions 2 through 4.

2. In two different ways, name a ray that starts at point *A* and goes to the right.

3. In two different ways, name a line segment that has points *C* and *B* as its endpoints.

4. In six different ways, name the line above.

5. How many different line segments can you name given the following information? (Note that $\overline{AB}$ and $\overline{BA}$ are the same line segment.)

a) a single point *A*

b) two points: *A* and *B*

c) three collinear points: *A*, *B* and *C*

d) four collinear points: *A*, *B*, *C* and *D*

e) five collinear points: *A*, *B*, *C*, *D* and *E*

f) What patterns do you notice?

Parallel and Perpendicular

Let's Review A plane is a two-dimensional space with infinite length and width but no thickness.

Perpendicular lines, line segments and rays meet or cross at a right angle and lie in the same plane.

Parallel lines lie in the same plane and never meet or cross. Parallel lines are always the same perpendicular distance apart.

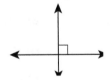

Use this diagram to answer Questions 6–11. As indicated by the small squares in the corners, lines meet at right angles at points A, C, E and G. Line segments $\overline{EA}$ and $\overline{CG}$ are the same length.

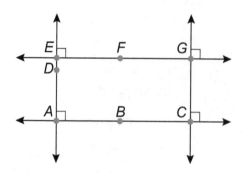

6. Name two rays that are perpendicular.

7. Name two line segments that are perpendicular.

8. Name two lines that are perpendicular.

9. Compare your answers to Questions 6, 7 and 8. What is alike and what is different?

10. Explain how you might draw a line that is parallel to any given line.

11. What shape is the polygon $AEGC$? Explain how you know.

12. **a)** If two lines, $\overleftrightarrow{AB}$ and $\overleftrightarrow{AD}$ lie in the same plane but are not parallel, must they intersect? When lines intersect they cross at a point.

    b) Two lines that are not parallel and do not intersect are called skew lines. Use rulers to represent lines and arrange them so they are skew. Explain in words how this is possible.

MATHEMATICALLY SPEAKING

▶ skew

13. Sketch each of the following, if possible. If it is not possible, explain why.

    a) three lines with 0 intersection points

    b) three lines with 1 point of intersection

    c) three lines with 2 intersection points

    d) three lines with 3 intersection points

    e) three lines with an infinite number of intersection points

⬆W rap It Up

ABCD is a rectangle.

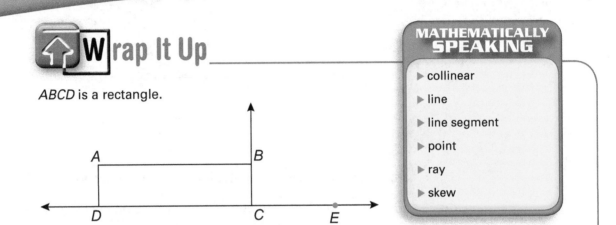

MATHEMATICALLY SPEAKING

▶ collinear

▶ line

▶ line segment

▶ point

▶ ray

▶ skew

Describe several relationships among the lines, line segments and rays using what you know about rectangles, parallel and perpendicular lines, line segments and rays.

Write About It

1. *ABCD* is a parallelogram. △*CED* is a right triangle.

   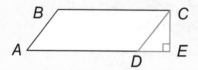

   a) Name two sets of parallel lines on the figure above.

   b) Name two perpendicular line segments on the figure above.

   c) Name two rays that form an obtuse angle.

   d) What shape is *ABCE*? How do you know?

2. Can a line be named by one letter, such as $\overleftrightarrow{C}$? Explain your reasoning.

3.

   a) Name the line above in three different ways.

   b) Name all possible line segments using the labels shown above. Note that $\overline{AB}$ and $\overline{BA}$ are the same line segment.

4. Sketch a polygon that is made of five line segments. Two of the segments should be parallel and a third line segment should be perpendicular to each of the parallel line segments. What shape have you drawn?

5. Sketch a polygon that has six congruent line segments in which each pair of opposite sides are parallel. What shape have you drawn?

6. **a)** Sketch three different polygons that have exactly one set of parallel sides and have no more than four sides. What shape is each of these?

   b) Sketch three different polygons that have exactly one set of parallel sides and have more than four sides. What shape is each of these?

7. Draw or trace a shape that matches each of the following:

   a) A quadrilateral with two sets of parallel line segments

   b) A pentagon with two line segments that are parallel to each other and perpendicular to a third line segment

   c) A triangle with two perpendicular line segments

   d) A hexagon with three sets of parallel line segments

   e) A regular polygon

8. a) Are the following rays parallel? Will they intersect?

   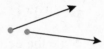

   b) Are the following lines parallel? Will they intersect?

   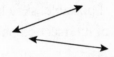

   c) Compare your answers to Parts a and b.

   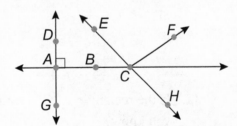

9. On the diagram above, which of the following is perpendicular to $\overleftrightarrow{BC}$?

   A. $\overline{DA}$ **C.** $\overline{GD}$

   B. $\overline{AG}$ **D.** All of the above

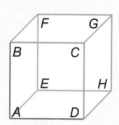

10. Think about two lines that lie in two separate planes. One example of this would be the lines represented by the edges of a cube.

a) Is it possible for the lines to intersect if they are in planes that do not intersect? Give an example using the edges of the cube.

b) Is it possible for the lines to lie in separate planes and not intersect? Give an example using the edges of the cube. Are these lines parallel?

c) State the definition of skew lines. Give an example of skew lines on the cube.

Think Beyond

11. If possible, sketch four lines resulting in the following total number of intersection points. If this is not possible, explain why it is not.

a) 0   d) 3   g) 6

b) 1   e) 4   h) 7

c) 2   f) 5   i) infinite

Think Back

12. Is the rectangle *ABCD* from Wrap It Up a parallelogram? How do you know?

13. a) A Cartesian coordinate grid is made of parallel and perpendicular lines. Locate the following points on the Cartesian grid like the one below and label them *A*, *B*, *C* and *D*. Draw line segments to connect points *A*, *B*, *C* and *D* in order. Then draw a line segment to connect point *D* to *A*.

A (4, 3); *B* (7, 3); *C* (7, 6); *D* (4, 6)

Justify each of your answers to the following.

b) Is the polygon *ABCD* a rectangle?

c) Is the polygon *ABCD* a rhombus?

d) Is the polygon *ABCD* a parallelogram?

e) Is the polygon *ABCD* a trapezoid?

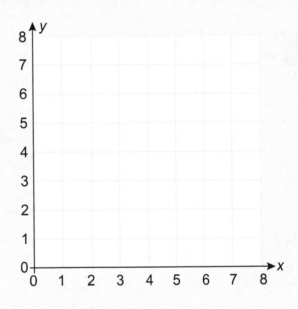

14. Which of the following is larger than $\frac{4}{9}$?

   A. $\frac{16}{36}$

   B. $\frac{20}{28}$

   C. $\frac{27}{72}$

   D. All of the above

   E. None of the above

15. Alison said that $\frac{4}{9}$ is larger than $\frac{4}{8}$ because 9 is larger than 8. Darius said that $\frac{4}{8}$ is larger than $\frac{4}{9}$ because eighths are larger than ninths.

   Who is right?

16. Find the perimeter of each polygon.

   a) an equilateral pentagon with sides of 2.36 cm

   b) a parallelogram with sides of $4\frac{1}{2}$ meters and $2\frac{2}{5}$ meters

   c) a scalene triangle with sides of $3\frac{1}{2}$ feet, $2\frac{1}{3}$ yards and 45 inches

LESSON 2.2 Name That Angle!

➡ Start It Off

Angle measurement is used to describe turns. The greater the amount of a turn, the larger the angle measurement.

1. Face the front of your classroom. If you turn your body a quarter turn clockwise, in what direction are you facing? What is the angle that you turned?

2. Face the front of your classroom. If you turn your body a half turn clockwise, in what direction are you facing? What is the angle that you turned?

3. Face the front of your classroom. If you turn your body a three-quarters turn clockwise, in what direction are you facing? What is the angle that you turned?

4. Face the front of your classroom. If you turn your body a full turn clockwise, in what direction are you facing? What is the angle that you turned?

5. Imagine making 2 complete turns. What is the angle measurement?

6. Make up some turning problems for your partner and determine the angle measurement.

Folding Angles

MATHEMATICALLY SPEAKING

▶ degree

When you learned about names of triangles, you used the ideas of acute, obtuse and right angles. You know that a corner of a rectangular sheet of paper is a right angle and measures 90 degrees. A degree is a unit that is used to measure the amount of turn in an angle.

1. Take a sheet of paper or patty paper and fold it to make angles of the following measures. Trace each one in your notes. Label the measure of each angle you trace.

   a) 45°   **b)** 22.5°

2. Use combinations of angles to make each of the following. Trace these in your notes. Label the measure of each angle traced and show the angles you combined to make it.

   a) 67.5°

   b) 180°

   c) 225°

   d) 135°

3. Take another sheet of paper or patty paper and fold it to show a 30° angle and a 60° angle. Trace these angles.

4. Use any of the angles you created to measure the amount of turn between the two hands of the clocks.

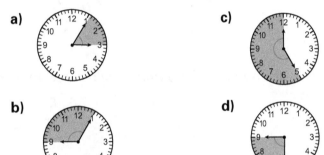

5. Are the following two angles congruent? Namely do they have the same measure? Explain.

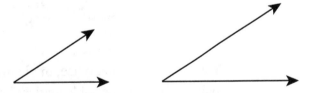

Naming Angles

MATHEMATICALLY
SPEAKING

▶ angle

▶ reflex angle

There are a number of ways to define an angle. An angle is the amount of a turn. An angle can also be defined as the figure formed by two rays with a common endpoint called a vertex.

The most common way to name an angle is either by using an upper case letter that names its vertex or by using three letters, one for a point on each ray that makes up the angle and one in the middle for its vertex. For example, the following angle might be named ∠A, ∠CAB or ∠BAC.

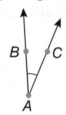

6. Name the following angle in three different ways.

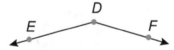

When you name an angle, you could be describing either angle between the rays.

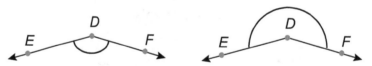

Unless it is noted otherwise, mathematicians are generally referring to the smaller of the two possible angles. The larger angle in the drawing above is called a reflex angle. A reflex angle is an angle with a measure greater than than 180° but less than 360°.

7. In the following, where is ∠A?

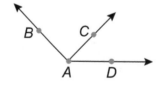

8. Why is it difficult to identify ∠A? How would you name the angles?

Measuring Angles

The measure of an angle is the amount of rotation from one ray to the other. Angles are based on the 360° found in a circle. One tool that can be used to measure angles is a protractor. You might have worked with a protractor before, or with another tool such as an angle ruler or goniometer.

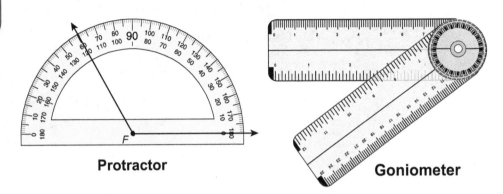

Protractor   **Goniometer**

Remember that a right angle has a measure of 90°, acute angles measure less than 90°, obtuse angles measure more than 90° but less than 180° and a straight angle has a measure of 180°. A complete turn consists of 360°.

Let's Review

Each protractor has a spot in the middle where you should place the vertex of the angle to be measured. It also has a line marked 0°. Draw an angle and place the center of the protractor on its vertex. Line up the protractor so one of the rays of the angle is on 0°. The number of degrees that the other ray goes through on the protractor is the measure of the angle. Note that you have two choices for the size of the angle. You should be able to determine which one to use based whether the size of the angle you are measuring is acute, obtuse, right or straight. Look at the protractor above. The protractor shows that the measure of the angle is either 60° or 120°. Use what you know about acute and obtuse angles to determine which of those is correct.

---

9. **a)** How do you use the type of the angle to help you decide which number to read?

   b) How would you find the measure of a reflex angle?

10. Look at the polygons in a set of Pattern Blocks.

    a) Estimate to locate a shape with a 60° angle. Check your estimate by measuring.

    b) Work with a partner and take turns estimating the sizes of other angles in the polygons in a set of Pattern Blocks. One of you should estimate and the other should measure to check the estimate. Record your results. Do your estimates get better after measuring a few angles?

11. Look at ∠*A* below.

    a) What is the measure of angle *A*?

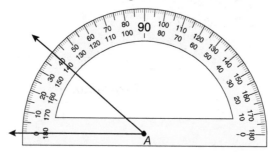

    b) How would you determine the number of degrees in the reflex angle at *A*?

12. Using a protractor and ruler, construct the following shapes.

    a) a square with side lengths of 4 cm

    b) a parallelogram that is not a rectangle

    c) a rhombus with 2 angle measures of 60° and 2 angle measures of 120°.

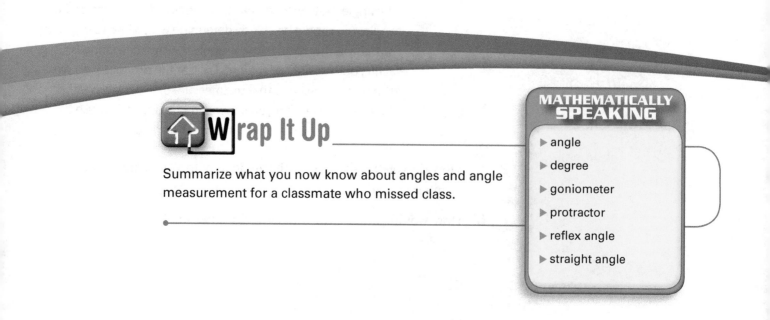

Wrap It Up

Summarize what you now know about angles and angle measurement for a classmate who missed class.

MATHEMATICALLY SPEAKING

- ▶ angle
- ▶ degree
- ▶ goniometer
- ▶ protractor
- ▶ reflex angle
- ▶ straight angle

Write About It

1. Winthrop thinks that the lengths of the rays that form an angle affect its measure. Namely an angle made from two short rays always measures less than one formed from two long rays. Ricky disagrees but hasn't come up with a convincing argument to explain why. Help Ricky explain to Winthrop why his reasoning isn't sound.

2. Draw angles with the following measures by folding and combining angles. Check your measurements using a protractor.

   a) 270°   **c)** 112.5°   **e)** 105°

   b) 225°   **d)** 67.5°   **f)** 75°

3. Tell whether each of the angles in Question 2 is acute, right, obtuse, straight or reflex.

4. Use a protractor or other measuring devise and draw angles with the following measures. Label the angles.

   a) 300°   **c)** 22°   **e)** 90°

   b) 85°   **d)** 130°   **f)** 165°

5. Measure the following angles.

   a)

   b)

   c)

6. **a)** What is the measure of a right angle?

   b) What is the measure of half of a right angle?

   c) What is the measure of two-thirds of a right angle?

   d) What is the measure of a straight angle?

   e) How many right angles does it take to make a complete circle?

7. **a)** Draw triangle *ABC*. Angle *A* should measure 45°, ∠*B* should measures 30°, and the side length, $\overline{AB}$, that connects the two angles, should be 5 cm long.

   b) Measure the third angle in your triangle and the length of the other two sides. Label your drawing.

   c) Draw a different triangle using the same information in Part a. How is it different from your first triangle?

8. **a)** Draw quadrilateral *WXYZ*. Make $m\angle W = 60°$, make $m\angle X = 30°$, and draw $\overline{WX}$ to connect the two angles so that the segment is 6 cm long.

   b) Measure the other two angles in your quadrilateral. Label your drawing. What is the sum of the four interior angles?

   c) Draw a different quadrilateral using the same information in Part a. How is it different from your first quadrilateral?

   d) Measure and label the two other angles in your quadrilateral from Part c. What is the sum of the four interior angles?

9. **a)** Suzanne has two brothers. Scott is 2 years younger than Suzanne and Dave is 9 years older than Suzanne. The sum of their three ages is 43 years. Let x represent Suzanne's age. Write an equation to represent the sum of their three ages.

    b) How old are the three siblings?

10. If 5 songs can be downloaded for $8, what is the cost of 7 songs?

11. Solve the following equations using any method. Show your work and check your solution.

    a) $4x - 20 = 28$ **b)** $-\frac{7}{8}y = 14$ **c)** $\frac{w}{3} = 10\frac{1}{2}$

12. Lionel agreed to do some gardening work for his uncle at a rate of $12 an hour. He worked for 3 hours. When he was done his aunt paid him and gave him a 15% tip rounded to the nearest dollar! How much money did Lionel make altogether?

13. An environmental firm is tracking temperatures during July in northern Alaska. They take a measurement every other day. Here are the 15 temperatures for the month of July in degrees Celsius.

3	14	8	10	12
15	11	9	12	12
13	10	7	8	7

    a) Find the median, first quartile (Q1) and third quartile (Q3).

    b) Create a box plot for the data.

    c) What is the interquartile range (IQR) for these data?

    d) Imagine you work for the firm. Write a statement about these data.

Complements, Supplements and Triangles

Start It Off

Use mental math to answer the following. Use your pencil only to record your answer.

1. 45 + _____ = 100
2. 45 + _____ = 90
3. 45 + _____ = 180
4. 45 + _____ = 360

5. 18 + _____ = 100
6. 18 + _____ = 90
7. 18 + _____ = 180
8. 18 + _____ = 360

9. 36 + _____ = 100
10. 36 + _____ = 90
11. 36 + _____ = 180
12. 36 + _____ = 360

What strategies do you use to find the missing addends? How can your answer to the first problem in each column help you find the answer to the other problems in that column?

13. Why are the numbers 90, 180 and 360 important when working with angles?

Angle Pairs

MATHEMATICALLY
SPEAKING

▶ complementary angles

▶ supplementary angles

Understanding how to measure and draw angles has prepared you to use these skills when working with pairs of angles. Two important angle pairs are complementary angles and supplementary angles. When the sum of the measures of two angles is 90°, the angles are called complementary angles. If the sum of the measures of two angles is 180°, the angles are called supplementary angles.

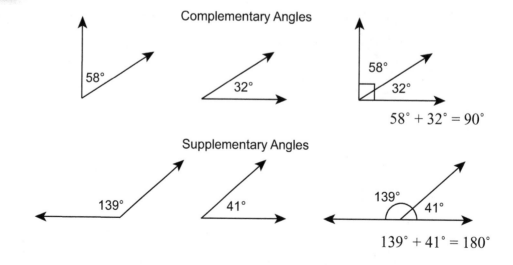

1. Knowing that two angles are complementary or supplementary means that if you know the measure of one angle, you can find the measure of the other angle without measuring.

   a) If you know the measure of one angle, how can you find the measure of an angle complementary to it?

   b) If you know the measure of one angle, how can you find the measure of an angle supplementary to it?

In the diagram below, line AB is perpendicular to line CD. This can be written in symbols as $\overleftrightarrow{AB} \perp \overleftrightarrow{CD}$. In this diagram, the measure of $\angle FED$ is 30° and $m\angle BEG = 45°$ ("$m\angle$" is mathematical shorthand for the measure of an angle).

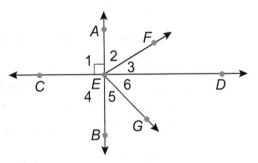

Note that angles may also be designated by a number inside the angle. In the diagram above, $\angle BEG$ may also be called $\angle 5$.

2. You now have all the information you need to determine the measures of all the other angles above. Using only the information given and without using a protractor, find the measure of each of the following. Unless otherwise noted, give the measure of the angle that is less than or equal to 180°, not the reflex angle.

   a) $\angle FEA$

   b) $\angle 6$

   c) $\angle CEG$

   d) $\angle AEG$

   e) $\angle AEG$ (reflex angle)

   f) $\angle FEC$

   g) $\angle FEG$

   h) $\angle GEF$ (reflex angle)

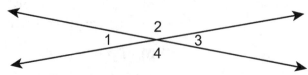

MATHEMATICALLY SPEAKING

▶ vertical angles

▶ adjacent angles

When two lines intersect, four angles are formed. A pair of angles that are opposite each other are said to be vertical angles. In the diagram below, angles 1 and 3 are vertical angles and angles 2 and 4 are vertical angles.

3. a) If you know the measure of ∠2, how would you find the measure of ∠3?

b) If you know the measure of ∠3, how would you find the measure of ∠4?

c) If you know the measure of ∠2, what do you know about the measure of ∠4? Explain.

4. Adjacent angles are two angles that share a common vertex and a common ray between them but do not overlap. Name two pairs of adjacent angles in the diagram above.

5. Write equations and then find the value of each variable in the following figures. Do not use a protractor. Instead use the properties of angles to help you. Write equations

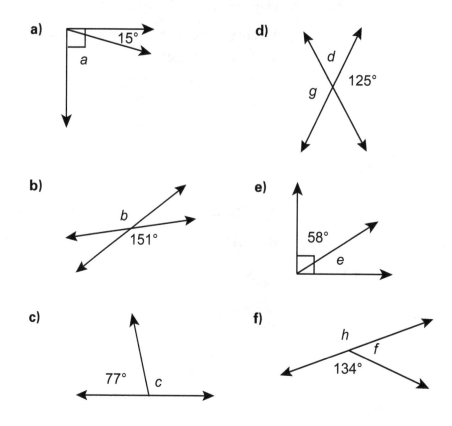

a) 15° a

d) d 125° g

b) b 151°

e) 58° e

c) 77° c

f) h f 134°

6. a) Determine the measure of all of the angles labeled with variables.

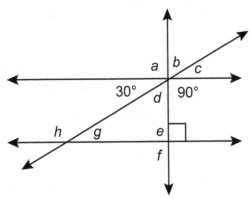

b) Name a pair of complementary angles.

c) Name a pair of supplementary angles.

d) Name a pair of vertical angles.

e) Name angles that form a straight angle.

Triangles

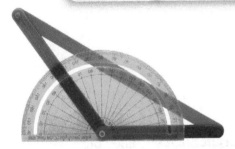

7. Use your AngLegs™ to construct a triangle. Estimate the size of each angle. Snap on the protractor to check your estimates.

8. a) Take an index card and use a ruler to draw a right triangle on the card. You might use the corner of the card for the right angle. The sides can be any length. Label the right angle as ∠1 and the other angles as ∠2 and ∠3. Cut out the triangle that you have drawn. Tear off the corners and rearrange them, placing the three angles together.

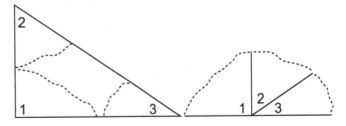

b) What can you say about the sum of the measures of the three angles from the triangle?

c) Repeat the process in Part a but with an acute scalene triangle. What do you notice about the angles?

d) Work with a partner. Each of you should repeat the process in Part a with three different types of triangles. What do you notice about the angles? Compare your results to your classmates.

e) What statement can you make about the sum of the measures of the angles of any triangle?

f) How does this compare to the sum of the measures of the angles of the triangle you built and measured using AngLegs™ in Question 7?

When constructing triangles you have to consider the angle measurements and the side lengths. So far, you have found that the sum of the angle measurements in any triangle is 180°. Does that mean that all triangles with the same angle measures are congruent? Lets investigate!

9. Work with a partner. Using a protractor and ruler or technology tool, draw triangles with the following angle measures. Remember to use markings to show when side lengths are the same.

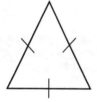 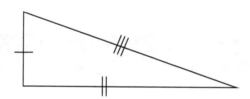

a) 90°, 45°, 45°

b) 60°, 60°, 60°

c) 120°, 50°, 10°

10. a) Compare triangles with the same angle measures that you and your partner drew. Are the triangles congruent? If not, what is the same about both triangles? What is different?

b) What generalizations can you make about triangles that have the same exact angle measures?

Let's also explore triangles with the same side lengths. If you are given three side lengths, how many triangles do you think you can make? Use AngLegs and a protractor to investigate. Copy the table below and answer the questions.

11.

Colors of AngLegs to Use	Number of Unique Triangles	Angle Measures in the Triangle(s)
a) Yellow, blue, red		
b) Blue, blue, blue		
c) Orange, purple, green		
d) Purple, purple, red		
e) Yellow, yellow, blue		
f) Orange, orange, purple		
g) Orange, purple, red		

12. a) Do all side lengths work to construct a triangle? Why or why not?

b) What else did you discover about triangles with specific side lengths?

13. In the following diagram *BCFE* is a rectangle and $m\angle D = 25°$. Find the measures of $\angle FCD$, $\angle BAC$ and $\angle ACB$ without using a protractor. Explain to a partner how you determined each measure.

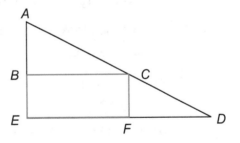

rap It Up

• If you know the three angle measurements of a triangle, is this enough information for everyone to draw the exact same triangle? Why or why not?

• If you know the three side lengths of a triangle, is this enough information for everyone to draw the exact same triangle? Why or why not?

MATERIALS LIST

▶ Protractor or goniometer

▶ AngLegs™

 **Write About It**

1. For the following, use diagrams and your best mathematical vocabulary to explain your reasoning.

   a) If you know that two adjacent angles are complementary, what do you know about the angle that is formed by combining them? If you know the measure of one of the angles, how would you find the measure of the complementary angle?

   b) If you know the measure of an angle, what do you know about the measure of its vertical angle?

   c) If you know the measure of an angle, how would you find the measure of its reflex angle?

2. a) Ella and Charlie were talking about triangles. Ella drew a triangle by first drawing a 40° angle, then a side of the triangle, and then a 120° angle. I know what the other angle will be without measuring, said Charlie. It will be _____ degrees.

   b) Ella stated: "I can make dozens of triangles with these angles." Do you agree or disagree with Ella? Explain.

3. Charlie then took three straws and experimented to see if they would make a triangle.

   a) Can you use any three lengths to always make a triangle? Why or why not?

   b) How many triangles can you make if you must use 3 specific lengths? Explain your thinking.

4. In the diagram below, $\overleftrightarrow{AB} \perp \overleftrightarrow{CD}$. The measure of $\angle FED$ is 40° and the measure of $\angle CEG$ is 15°.

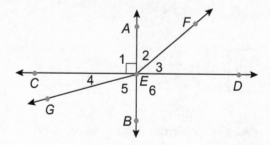

   a) Name two pairs of adjacent complementary angles.

   b) Name one pair of supplementary angles. Are the angles adjacent?

   c) Name one pair of vertical angles. What is the measure of each?

5. Fill in the chart below using the diagram in Question 4. Complete the chart noting the measurement and type of angle. Use only the information given and do not use a protractor. The first one is completed for you.

Angle	Angle Number(s)	Measure of Angle that is Less than or Equal to 180°	Measure of Reflex Angle	Type of Angle that is ≤ 180° (Acute, Obtuse, Right or Straight)
∠AEG	1, 4	105°	255°	Obtuse angle
∠BEG				
∠FEC				
∠GED				
∠FEB				
∠AEB				
		130°		
			345°	

6. a) Use AngLegs and construct three triangles and three quadrilaterals and estimate the measure of each angle in each polygon. Measure to check your estimates. Then find the sum of the measures of the angles in each polygon.

Color of AngLegs to Make Triangle	Estimates for Measures of Angles	Actual Measures of Angles	Sum of Measures of Angles

Colors of AngLegs to Make Quadrilaterals	Estimates for Measures of Angles	Actual Measures of Angles	Sum of Measures of Angles

b) What do you notice about the sum of the angle measures in the triangles? How does this compare to your discoveries from tearing angles on a triangle?

c) What do you notice about the sum of the angle measures in the quadrilaterals? Measure other types of quadrilaterals made with AngLegs™ to see if the same thing is true.

7. Draw any quadrilateral on an index card and cut it out.

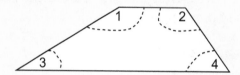

a) Tear off the four corners and put them together.

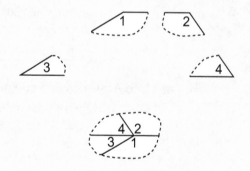

b) What can you say about sum of the measure of the four angles from the quadrilateral?

c) Do the same thing for a parallelogram. What can you say about the sum of the measure of the angles?

d) Do the same for three different types of quadrilaterals. Include at least one quadrilateral with obtuse angles. What do you notice about the angles?

e) How does this compare to what you found when you measured the angles of a quadrilateral in a set of pattern blocks?

f) What generalization can you make about the sum of the angles of any quadrilateral?

8. Using only the fact that m ∠1 is 30° and ∠2 is a right angle, find the measure of each of the other numbered angles. Do not use a protractor.

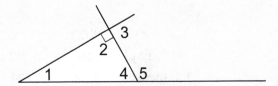

a) m∠3 = _____

b) m∠4 = _____

c) m∠5 = _____

9. Figure *ABCD* is a parallelogram.

m∠1 = m∠6 = 50°; m∠2 = m∠8 = 90°. Find the measure of each of the other angles and explain your thinking.

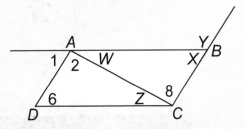

Angle	Measure	Explanation
∠W		
∠X		
∠Y		
∠Z		

10. Use what you know about complementary, supplementary and vertical angles; the sum of the angles in a triangle; and parallel and perpendicular lines to make up a puzzle about angle measures and trade with a classmate.

Think Beyond

11. You know that the sum of the measures of the angles of a triangle is 180°. Explain how you might use this information to find the sum of the measures of the angles of any pentagon. Show your method on a concave pentagon and a convex pentagon.

Think Beyond

12. Your brother, who is taking geometry in high school, has told you that the opposite angles of any parallelogram (the angles opposite each other, such as ∠1 and ∠5 in the figure below) are congruent. In the figure below, you know that ∠1 has a measure of 30° and $ED \perp CD$. Use this information to help you find the measure of each of the other angles in the diagram. Explain your thinking.

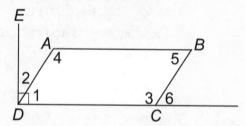

Angle	Measure	Explanation
∠2		
∠3		
∠4		
∠5		
∠6		

13. When a ball hits a wall in miniature golf, it bounces off the wall at the same angle at which it hit the wall.

a) In the diagram below, the ball is bouncing off the wall and going into the hole for a "hole-in-one." Estimate the measure of ∠1 and ∠2 and then check your estimate by measuring.

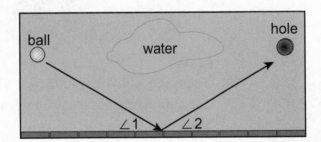

b) For each of the following holes, first estimate the measures of the angle at which the ball must hit for you to make a "hole-in-one." After you have estimated, copy the diagram into your notebook and use your protractor to draw the angles of your estimates. Did you hit the hole?

Hole	Estimate for Angles	Hole-in-One?
1		
2		
3		

Hole 1

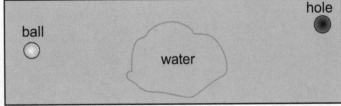

Hole 2

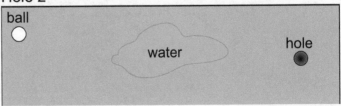

Hole 3

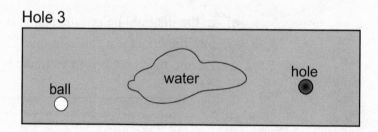

14. The National Library of Virtual Manipulatives has a number of intriguing activities using angle measures. Try some of the Ladybug Mazes at this site.

15. In the following diagram, $\overleftrightarrow{AD} \perp \overleftrightarrow{BC}$. The measure of $\angle 1$ is 35°. What is the measure of each of the other numbered angles?

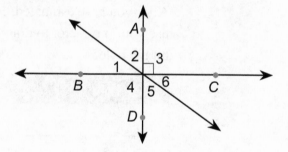

16. Miniature golf costs $5.00 for each adult and $3.50 for each person under the age of 18. The Gabbard family paid $27.00 to play miniature golf. How many people in the family were adults and how many were under 18? Show your work.

17. After miniature golf, the Gabbards went out for pizza. The pizza parlor has:

    • Thick, thin or stuffed crust

    • Pepperoni, sausage or ham

    a) The Gabbards decided to select one choice from each category. How many different ways might they do this? Show your work.

    b) If the Gabbards also choose either mushrooms or peppers, how many total different combinations would be possible? How did you figure this out?

18. The Gabbards went to a science museum. They drove 95 miles each way. Their car gets 19 miles per gallon and gas cost $3.14 per gallon. How much did gas cost for the trip? Show your work.

19. The Gabbards bought two books from the museum gift shop at $19.85 each and a solar kit for $28.32. These amounts included tax. How much change did they get back from $70.00? Show your work.

20. Later, when the Gabbards were in a mall bookstore, they saw one of the books that they just bought from the science museum priced at $25.00 below a sign that read "25% off, includes tax." The book at the Science Museum was $19.85 including tax. Which book was the better buy?

Optional Technology Lesson for this section available in your eBook

Sum It Up

In this section, you learned some basic geometric ideas including concepts of angles and how they are measured.

Points, Lines and Rays

- Points, lines and rays were defined by a Greek mathematician named Euclid over 2000 years ago. Many geometric concepts are built from these basic ideas.

- A point is a location in space that has no length, width or height. A line or line segment has one dimension, length, but no width or height. A plane and plane figures like polygons and circles have only two dimensions: length and width.

- Parallel lines never meet and are always the same distance apart.

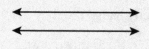

parallel lines

- Perpendicular lines, rays and line segments meet at a 90° angle.

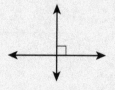

perpendicular lines

- If two lines or two segments are skew, they do not intersect and they are not parallel. Skew lines or skew segments are in different planes. In the diagram, segments $\overline{AB}$ and $\overline{CG}$ are skew.

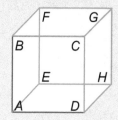

Angles

- Angle measures are based on the 360 degrees found in a circle and can be measured by a protractor or goniometer.

- The measure of a right angle is 90° and the measure of a straight angle is 180°. The sum of the measures of a pair of complementary angles is 90° and the sum of the measures of a pair of supplementary angles is 180°.

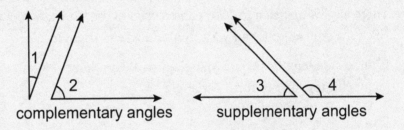

complementary angles   supplementary angles

- Adjacent angles are two angles that share a common vertex and a common ray between them. They do not overlap. Angles 5 and 6 (below) are adjacent angles.

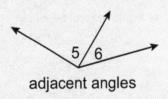

adjacent angles

- Vertical angles are the angles opposite each other that are formed by two intersecting lines. They share a common vertex and are congruent. In the diagram below, angles 1 and 3 are vertical angles. Angles 2 and 4 are also vertical angles.

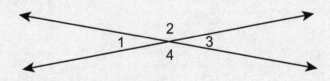

- The sum of the measures of the angles of a triangle is 180°. This can be shown by cutting out any type of triangle, tearing off the three corners and lining them up so they form a straight angle.

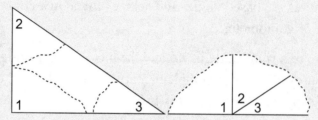

- Three angles that sum to 180° can be used to draw a triangle but not a unique triangle since the side lengths can vary from triangle to triangle.

- If three side lengths form a triangle, it will be unique. Not all combinations of 3 side lengths fit together to form a triangle.

MATHEMATICALLY SPEAKING

Do you know what these mathematical terms mean?

- adjacent angles
- angle
- collinear
- complementary angles
- degree
- goniometer

- line
- line segment
- point
- protractor
- ray
- reflex angle

- skew
- straight angle
- supplementary angles
- vertical angles

Part 1. What did you learn?

1. Two adjacent angles, ∠1 and ∠2, form a right angle.

   a. Are these angles supplementary, complementary, vertical or perpendicular?

   b. How would you find the measure of ∠2 if you know the measure of ∠1?

2. Lines $\overleftrightarrow{AB}$ and $\overleftrightarrow{BC}$ are perpendicular. Line $\overleftrightarrow{DE}$ intersects both lines, but is not perpendicular to line $\overleftrightarrow{AB}$ or line $\overleftrightarrow{BC}$.

   a. Sketch a diagram that meets this description.

   b. Record the names of two perpendicular rays.

   c. Record the names of two intersecting, but non-perpendicular, line segments.

3. If ∠1 measures less than 180° and ∠2 is the reflex angle to ∠1, explain how you would find the measure of ∠2.

4. Find the measure of ∠ABC below. Explain how you found it.

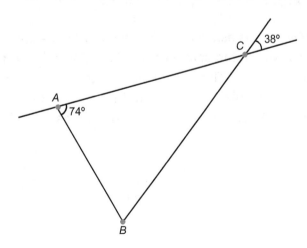

5. **a.** Draw a triangle that is composed of a right angle and an angle that is the complementary angle to 35°.

b. What is the measure of the third angle in your triangle?

c. How many triangles can you draw with these exact same angle measurements? Explain.

d. Measure the side lengths in centimeters and label your drawing. How many unique triangles can you draw with these exact side lengths?

6. In the figure below, $\angle 1$ measures 85°, $\angle 3$ measures 108° and $\angle 4$ measures 30°. Find the measure of $\angle 2$.

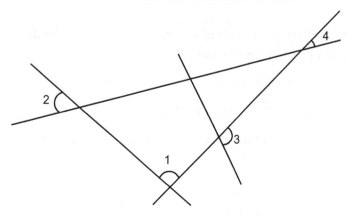

7. On a recent quiz, Martin was asked to look at a pair of lines and explain whether they were intersecting or parallel. Martin looked at the lines below and wrote, "These are neither intersecting nor parallel. They are perpendicular. They are not intersecting but they touch at a right angle." What is wrong with Martin's reasoning?

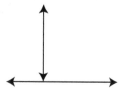

Area, Surface Area and Volume

Polyhedrons are everywhere! Books, rooms, containers for food and drink, and boxes are examples of objects that can be classified as polyhedrons. How much will fit into a container or how much material is needed to wrap it will be the focus in this section.

When a company plans to sell a product, it must decide on the amount of the product to place in each package. The company must also decide on how it will package the product. Will the item fit into a box or a bag? What will the packaging look like? How much will it cost? As you work through these lessons, you will have an opportunity to answer similar questions and use your understanding of area, surface area and volume.

 LESSON 3.1 Circumference

 **Start It Off**

1. What do you know about circles? Brainstorm with a partner and write three facts.

2. Talk with your partner. How might you define a circle? Write a definition.

3. What tool is used to draw a circle?

4. Draw 4 concentric circles. Concentric circles have the same center point.

MATHEMATICALLY SPEAKING

▶ concentric

MATHEMATICALLY SPEAKING

▶ center (of a circle)
▶ chord
▶ circle
▶ diameter
▶ radius (radii)

Let's Review A circle is the set of points that are all the same distance from one point, the center. The circle below is called Circle O. A radius of a circle is the distance from the center of the circle to any point on the circle. The radius is also defined as a line segment with one endpoint at the center of the circle and the other endpoint on a point on the circle. When you have more than one radius, they are called *radii*.

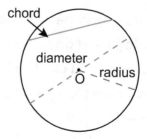

A chord of a circle is a line segment that joins any two points on the circle. A diameter of a circle is a chord that goes through the center. We also use the term, diameter, for the length of these chords.

1. Compare the length of a diameter of a circle to the length of a radius of the same circle. What do you notice?

2. How many diameters do you think are in a circle? Explain.

Investigating Circumference

MATHEMATICALLY SPEAKING

▶ circumference

The perimeter of a circle has a special name, the circumference of the circle. Circumference is a length; it is measured using units such as inches, feet, miles, millimeters, centimeters and meters.

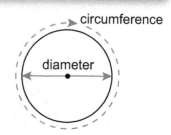

3. **a)** How long is the circumference of common circular objects such as a frisbee, a lid of a plastic container, or your wrist? Let's investigate! First, estimate the length of the circumference of a frisbee.

   b) Use a piece of tape to mark the rim of the frisbee. Also place a piece of tape on the floor as your starting point. Line up the two marks and roll the frisbee a complete turn to determine the length of the circumference. What is its length? (don't forget the units!)

c) Estimate the circumference of a circular plastic lid or some other object in your classroom. Then measure to find the exact circumference.

d) Estimate the circumference of your ankle, wrist, head and neck. Use string and a tape measure to determine the actual circumference.

e) Did your estimates improve? What information helped you refine your estimates?

The ratio of the circumference of a circle to its diameter is a proportional relationship. You have explored many proportional relationships so far in *Math Innovations*.

4. **a)** Work with a partner to measure the circumference and diameter of 7 circular objects. Measure these lengths to the nearest tenth of a centimeter. You can use the measurements from the frisbee and the plastic lid as two of your objects. Record these data in a table similar to the one below.

Objects	Circumference (*C*)	Diameter (*d*)	Circumference : Diameter
Frisbee			
Plastic lid			

b) Find the value of the ratio of circumference to diameter ($C:d$) for each of your circular objects. Round each value to hundredths. What do you notice?

c) Compare the value(s) you found for the ratio to the value(s) other students found. Why are everyone's values about the same, but not exactly the same? What number is the constant of proportionality?

d) What should the graph of a proportional relationship look like? Use this information and your data to sketch a graph of the relationship between circumference and diameter. Place diameter on the *x*-axis and circumference on the *y*-axis.

The ratio between circumference and diameter in all circles is the number known as π. Mathematicians have been fascinated by pi (π) for thousands of years and have developed techniques to compute its value to high degrees of accuracy. It is an irrational number; this means there is no way to write it as a fraction using integers. The decimal representation for π goes on indefinitely. The first 30 decimal places are shown to the right. Pi is often rounded to 3.14.

$$\pi$$

3.141592653589793238462643383279

5. Sometimes directions in math problems say to use $\frac{22}{7}$ to represent π.

   a) What is the decimal equivalent of $\frac{22}{7}$?

   b) Is $\frac{22}{7}$ equal to π? Why or why not?

6. a) Let's say you knew the diameter of a circle. How would you calculate the circumference of the circle?

   b) What if you only knew the radius of a circle. Is it possible to calculate the circumference? How?

   c) Imagine that you knew the circumference of a circle. Discuss with your partner how you would find the diameter of the circle.

Circle Problems

Now that you are aware of the proportional relationship between circumference and diameter, you can use it to solve problems. There are two equivalent formulas for circumference: $C = \pi d$ and $C = 2\pi r$.

7. a) Why are these two formula equivalent?

   b) What value should be used for π? What is the value on your calculator?

Remember that when solving problems that use formulas, it is a good idea to first write down the formula that you will be using. Then on the next line, write an equation where you have substituted values for the variables in the equation. Don't forget to enter an approximate value for π. Next, solve for the unknown value. Don't forget to label your answer.

Imagine you have 50 yards of fencing to put around a circular vegetable garden. You plan to use all 50 yards of fencing. What is the diameter of the biggest circular garden you can make?

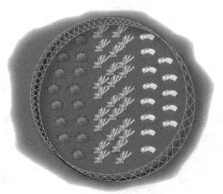

$$C = \pi d$$
$$50 = 3.14 \cdot d$$
$$50 \div 3.14 = d$$
$$15.9 \approx d$$

Note: You need to choose an approximate value for π. You can use 3.14 or $\frac{22}{7}$.

Note: Since 3.14 is an approximate value for π, the value for d is also approximate.

8. In the midwest, irrigation is used to water crops. One type of sprinkler system is designed to spray water is a circle. The reach of the water from the sprinkler head to the crops is 40 feet. What is the length of the circumference of these giant circles?

9. Imagine a cross section of the Earth that goes right through the equator. It forms a circle. The diameter of the Earth has been measured by scientists to be approximately 7926 miles. If we assume that the Earth is a perfect sphere (which it isn't), then what is the circumference at the equator of the Earth?

10. Vinyl records were the primary way people listened to music in the 20th century. A record has an inscribed spiral groove that starts at the outside of the record and ends at the center. If the outside groove of a record from the 1960s is $37\frac{5}{8}$ inches long, what is the radius of the record?

circumference $37\frac{5}{8}$

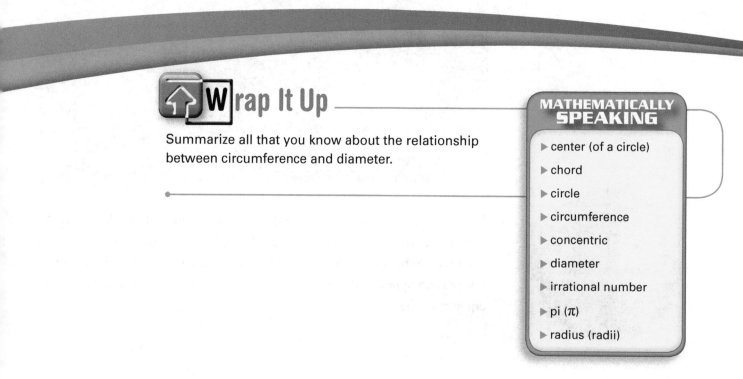

Wrap It Up

Summarize all that you know about the relationship between circumference and diameter.

MATHEMATICALLY SPEAKING

▶ center (of a circle)

▶ chord

▶ circle

▶ circumference

▶ concentric

▶ diameter

▶ irrational number

▶ pi (π)

▶ radius (radii)

 **Write About It**

1. There is a lot of mathematical vocabulary in this lesson. Make a small poster, flash cards, or a review sheet that defines each term and includes an illustration. For three of the vocabulary words also write a sentence that uses the vocabulary word in a way that will help you remember the meaning.

2. Estimate the circumference or diameter for each of the following circles.

   a) The radius is 3 cm. What is the circumference?

   b) The diameter is 20 inches. What is the circumference?

   c) The circumference is 1 mile. What is the diameter?

   d) The circumference is 3.14 ft. What is the diameter?

   e) Explain your reasoning for Part c.

3. Kendra was doing some calculations and found the circumference of a circle. She wrote her answer as $C = 2.5\pi$ cm. Paul calculated the circumference of the same circle but wrote $C \approx 7.85$ cm. Their teacher marked both of their answers correct.

   a) How can it be that both are correct?

   b) Is either of their answers the "better" answer? Explain.

4. A clock for a large wall is being built. It will have a wood rim around the outer edge. The diameter will be 24 inches. How long will the wood rim need to be?

5. What is the circumference of the largest circle that can be cut from a square that is 18 inches wide?

6. The shape below is composed of a rectangle and a semi-circle (half of a circle). Calculate the perimeter of the shape.

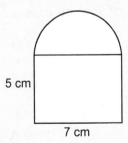

5 cm

7 cm

7. Which is longer? The perimeter of a rectangle that is 18 cm by 16 cm or the perimeter of a circle with a diameter of 15 cm? Explain your reasoning.

8. Find the missing values for the three different circles.

   a) $r = \frac{8}{14}$ inch

   Find C.

   b) $C = 7.54$ cm

   Find r.

   c) $d = 19$ mm

   Find C and r.

9. Summer camps often have craft activities for the campers. One craft activity is to make woven bracelets and necklaces. Make up two problems that use the math concepts from this lesson. Solve your problems.

10. Bean bag toss games are commonly found at fairs and carnivals. The idea is to toss a bean bag through a small hole from a considerable distance. If the hole in the target below is $15\frac{3}{4}$ inches around, what is the approximate diameter of the hole?

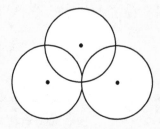 **Think Beyond**

11. Three circles, each with a radius of 4 cm are combined. Find the circumference (distance around the outside) of this new shape.

Healthy Grains
High Fiber

O's

Volume:
72 cubic cm

12. **a)** The fraction $\frac{4}{5}$ can mean different things depending on the interpretation. Fractions can represent divisions, parts of a whole, measurements and ratios. Pick two of the interpretations and explain what $\frac{4}{5}$ represents based on each.

b) Draw pictures to illustrate your answer to Question 12a.

13. What is the rule for where to place the decimal point when you multiply two decimal numbers such as 4.5 and 3.6? Explain why this rule works.

14. In the cereal box to the left, what is the relationship among the number of edges, faces and vertices?

15. Evaluate and simplify: $\dfrac{\left(\frac{1}{2} + \frac{9}{5}\right)}{2}$

16. **a)** Define the following terms: *factor*, *product*, *quotient*, *divisor* and *dividend*.

b) How are these terms related?

Area of Circles

➡ Start It Off

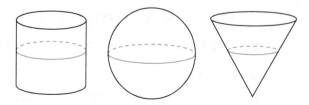

1. Earlier in this unit, you explored cross sections of prisms and pyramids. Imagine taking a cross section of the solids above by slicing them horizontally. What shapes are the cross sections of the cylinder, sphere and cone?

2. Imagine slicing the three solids vertically. Are any of these cross sections circles? Why or why not?

3. The diameter of a cross section of a cylinder is 7 cm. What is the circumference of the cylinder?

4. The cross section of a tree truck that is in the shape of a cylinder has a radius of 6 inches. What is the circumference of the tree?

5. In some towns when a tree on public land dies, it is replaced by a tree of equal size. If a tree that has a circumference of about 62.8 inches needs to be replaced, what is the radius of the replacement tree?

Making Sense of Circles

Pizza is traditionally made in the shape of a circle. When you order a pizza, you pick its size based on your appetite or on the number of people sharing. But how much pizza is in a large or small pizza? The area of a pizza measures the size of its surface.

One way to estimate the area of a pizza is to use a grid. First, count the number of squares covered by one piece of pizza. Then, multiply that number by the total number of pieces. Let's use this method to find the area of a pizza with a 7-inch radius that has been cut into 8 slices. First, count the number of complete squares that are covered by the pizza slice. Then combine parts of squares that are covered by the slice to make whole squares. Estimate the number of complete squares that can be made from all of the pieces. Using this method, the approximate number of square inches covered by the pizza slice is 19.

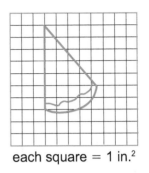

Area of $\frac{1}{8}$ of the pizza ≈ 19 in.^{2}

Area of circle $\approx 8 \cdot 19$

≈ 152 in.^{2}

each square = 1 in.^{2}

The area of a pizza with a radius of 7 inches is approximately 152 square inches. As you can see, counting square units is not an efficient way to measure area.

Understanding the Area Formula

Another way to find the area of a pizza is to use the formula for the area of a circle. We develop this formula below.

- Draw a circle. Next, cut the circle out, and finally cut it into 16 wedges.

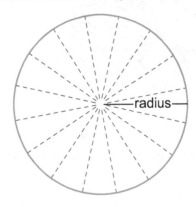

- Rearrange the wedges to form a pattern similar to the one below. The shape that you have made is almost a parallelogram. Tape your parallelogram onto a piece of paper.

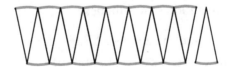

- Only half of the circle is used for the base. This means the base of the parallelogram is half the circumference.

$C = 2\pi r$ 　　Base of parallelogram $= \frac{2\pi r}{2}$ or πr

- On your drawing of the parallelogram, label the base and the height using the variable r.

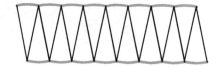

- Find the area of the parallelogram. Use the formula $A = b \cdot h$.

$$A_{parallelogram} \approx A_{circle} = \pi r \cdot r \quad \text{or} \quad A_{circle} = \pi r^2$$

1. Are the areas of the circle and the parallelogram the same? Explain.

2. Explain why the base of the parallelogram is half of $2\pi r$.

3. Why did we use $C = 2\pi r$ instead of $C = \pi d$ to find the base of the parallelogram?

4. Why is the radius squared (r^2) in the formula for area of a circle?

5. Use the formula to find the area of the large pizza at the beginning of the lesson. Use $\frac{22}{7}$ as an approximate value for π. Compare the result to the one you obtained by Method 1.

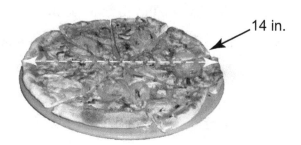

14 in.

What if you want to purchase the most pizza for your money? The pizza that costs the least per square inch is the best buy. Use 3.14 as an approximate value for π.

6. **a)** The diameter of a small pizza is 10 inches. The diameter of a medium pizza is 12 inches. How much larger is the medium pizza than the small pizza?

   b) How does the area of the medium pizza compare to the large pizza with a radius of 7 inches?

   c) The small pizza costs $7.00, the medium costs $10.50, and the large pizza costs $12.50. Which pizza costs the least per square inch?

When you calculate with π, the numerical answer will always be an approximation because π is rounded (to either 3.14 or $\frac{22}{7}$). To find the area of a pizza, with a 10-inch diameter:

$A = \pi r^2$

$A \approx 3.14 \cdot 5^2$

$A \approx 3.14 \cdot 25$

$A \approx 78.5$ in.^{2} This answer is an approximation of the area of the pizza.

The sign for "is approximately" is ≈.

Mathematicians sometimes do not use a value for π in order to give an exact answer.

$A = \pi r^2$

$A = \pi \cdot 5^2$

$A = 25\pi$ in.^{2} This answer is the exact area of the pizza.

7. Explain why an answer is exact when you do not give a value to π when calculating.

 **W rap It Up**

Stuart said: "When you cut a circle into four wedges and put them together, they don't really look like a parallelogram. But when you cut a circle into lots of wedges, it looks more like a parallelogram. With lots of wedges it is easier to understand the formula for the area of a circle." What do you think Stuart meant by this comment? Why did lots of wedges help him understand the formula?

NOTE Use 3.14 or $\frac{22}{7}$ for π. Round final answers to the nearest tenth.

Write About It

1. Benedict confuses the area and circumference formulas of circles. Write what you know about the meaning of these two measurements. What variables are important? How do you remember the formulas for the area and circumference of circles?

2. **a)** The radius of the wagon wheel is 14 inches. What is the area of the wagon wheel?

   b) What is the area between two spokes of the wheel?

3. Station WSEB can be heard on the radio as far as 60 miles from its transmitter. To the nearest ten square miles, how many square miles does the station serve?

4. Italy uses the metric system. Pizza in Italy is measured using centimeters, not inches. The area of one Italian pizza is 132 cm².

   a) Find the radius of this pizza.

   b) Look at a ruler that has inches and centimeters on it. Is the Italian pizza closer in size to the small, medium or large pizza mentioned in the lesson?

5. The Super Spreader Sprinkler is a circular sprinkler that waters 700 ft.² of lawn. Tara bought a Super Spreader Sprinkler for her dad on Father's Day. If she does not want the water from the sprinkler to hit the house, how far away does she need to place it?

6. Stonehenge is a monument in Southern England made of large stones arranged in an outer circle and an inner circle. These stones are within a larger circle bounded by a ditch and an outer bank. From 2950–2900 B.C.E., this monument covered a large circular area with a circumference measuring 314.15 meters. How much space did the Stonehenge monuments cover during this time?

7. What are the advantages of using a formula to find the area of a circle over counting squares?

8. Find the area of the following figure.

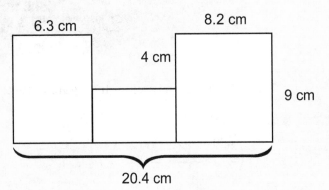

6.3 cm

8.2 cm

4 cm

9 cm

20.4 cm

9. Mary Elizabeth and her six friends went out for pizza. Three of them wanted pepperoni while the others wanted pineapple. The price for two 9-inch diameter pizzas or one 18-inch diameter pizza is the same. Mary Elizabeth wants to make sure both options buy the same amount of pizza. Which should they order?

10. Find the missing values.

    a) $A = 42\frac{1}{4}\pi$ m²

        $r = ?$

    b) $C \approx 5.7$ mm²

        $r = ?$

    c) $A \approx 196$ cm²

        $C \approx ?$

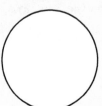

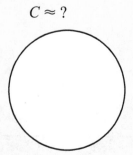

    d) When is the area of a circle an exact value and when is it an approximation?

11. A circular fountain has a diameter of 20 ft. There is a surrounding bench that is 2.5 ft. wide. What is the area of the bench?

20 ft.

2.5 ft.

12. Determine the area of the figure below.

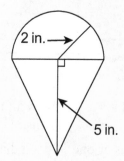

2 in.

5 in.

13. Compact discs are made out of polycarbonate plastic. Most CDs have a diameter of 120 mm. There is a small hole with a diameter of 15 mm in the middle of all CDs. In order for a musical album to be certified platinum in the United States, it must sell one million copies. If an album is certified platinum, how many square millimeters of polycarbonate plastic were used to make one million CDs? How many square meters?

14. **a)** The figure below is made up of two circles, one with a radius of 1 cm and the other with a radius of 2 cm. Find the area of the shaded part. Use 3.14 as an approximation for pi.

   b) Find the difference in the circumference of the two circles in terms of π.

15. Find the area of the shaded region.

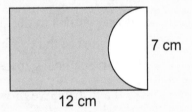

7 cm

12 cm

Think
Back

16. Find the missing values in each table.

a)

Input	Output
1	$\frac{3}{2}$
2	3
3	$\frac{9}{2}$
4	6
10	
11	
	21

b)

Input	Output
5	$\frac{5}{8}$
8	1
13	$1\frac{5}{8}$
24	3
1	
−4	
	$\frac{7}{8}$
	$1\frac{1}{2}$

17. If a prism and a pyramid have the same size base, how are the number of edges they each have related?

18. A flower garden in the shape of a trapezoid has an area of 54 yd². The lengths of the two bases are 9 yd and 15 yd. What is the height of the trapezoidal garden?

19. Use the distributive property to simplify the following expression:

$28(93) + 28(7)$

20. Examine the stem-and-leaf plot of the scores from a class of 7th grade students on a recent science test.

```
9 | 7 5
8 | 9 8 8 6 5 5 2 1 0 0 0
7 | 9 9 9 7 3 1
6 | 8
5 | 2
```

a) What part of the graph is the "stem?"

b) What part of the graph are the "leaves?"

c) Describe the data in terms of the achievement of the class.

d) What was the median test score? Explain how you found it.

Surface Area of Rectangular Prisms

➡️ Start It Off

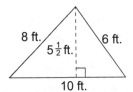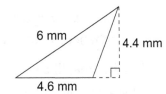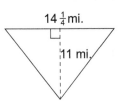

1. Find the areas of the triangles. Do not use a calculator.

2. Explain why the area formula for a triangle works.

3. To find the areas of the triangles above, Rex used $A = \frac{bh}{2}$, while Phuong used $A = \frac{1}{2}bh$. Explain why these two formulas are equivalent using words and symbols.

Packaging is an important part of product design. People are attracted to items that are in interesting boxes and containers. Some companies design and produce all types of boxes like the CD box you experimented with in Section 1. There is a lot of math involved in packaging!

Understanding Surface Area

The amount of cardboard that forms all the faces of a box is known as the surface area of the box. In general, surface area is the total area of all of the faces of an object. We can also think of surface area as the amount of material needed to cover or wrap the outside of a space figure.

1. List three everyday three-dimensional objects. Give reasons why you might need to measure the surface area of each object.

Surface area, like area, is measured in square units, such as square inches, square feet, square meters and square centimeters. These square units are abbreviated by raising the unit to the second power (unit^2, in.^{2}, ft.^{2}, m^2, and cm^2).

2. Why is area measured using square units, such as square centimeters, rather than linear units, such as centimeters?

One way to calculate the surface area of a prism is to use orthogonal views and find the area of each face.

3. Draw orthogonal views of the top, front and side views of each rectangular prism. Label each view with its dimensions.

a)

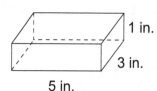

1 in.
3 in.
5 in.

c)

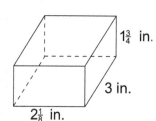

$1\frac{3}{4}$ in.
3 in.
$2\frac{1}{8}$ in.

b)

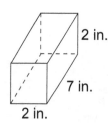

2 in.
7 in.
2 in.

d)

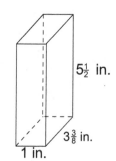

$5\frac{1}{2}$ in.
$3\frac{3}{8}$ in.
1 in.

4. Determine the surface area of each of the rectangular prisms in Question 3.

5. Wilhem complained that it took a while to calculate the surface area of the rectangular prisms. "I had to find the area of each of the six faces and then add those together." Describe a more efficient method of finding the surface area of a rectangular prism. Use Question 3c to explain.

6. Here is a rectangular prism where the measurements of the dimensions are unknown. The variable *l* represents the length, *w* represents the width and *h* represents the height.

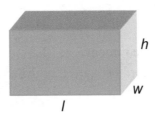

a) Sketch the front, top and side views of this prism and write the area of each face using the appropriate variables.

b) Use your results from Part a to write a rule for finding the surface area of a rectangular prism.

7. a) Lianne uses the formula $SA = 2lw + 2lh + 2wh$ to find the surface area of rectangular prisms. Victor uses the formula $SA = 2(lw + lh + wh)$. What do the numbers and the symbols (SA, lw, lh, wh, 2) represent in these formulas?

b) Are the formulas equivalent? Why or why not?

Wrap It Up

When you find the surface area of a rectangular prism, it is important to write the formula and then clearly record the calculations. Why is this important? What can you do to record your work more precisely? Demonstrate your ideas by determining the surface area of the following rectangular prisms.

MATHEMATICALLY SPEAKING

▶ surface area

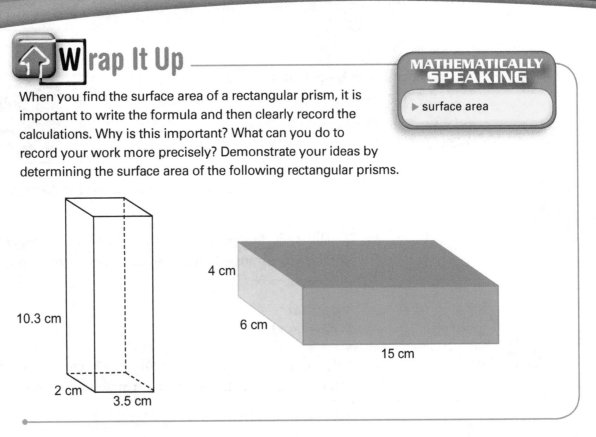

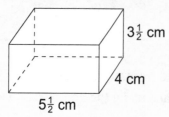

Write About It

1. Explain how the dimensions of a rectangular prism are used to determine its surface area. Use the example below.

$3\frac{1}{2}$ cm

4 cm

$5\frac{1}{2}$ cm

2. Think about the orthogonal views of a cube. Develop a simple formula for finding the surface area of a cube. Make sure your formula works for all cubes.

3. Find the surface area of the following prisms.

a)

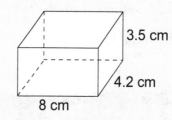

3.5 cm

4.2 cm

8 cm

b)

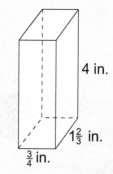

4 in.

$1\frac{2}{3}$ in.

$\frac{3}{4}$ in.

4. Sam bought his brother a basketball for his birthday and needs to wrap it. The basketball is in a box in the shape of a cube that has 15-inch edges.

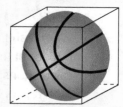

a) How much wrapping paper is needed to exactly cover all surfaces of the box?

b) Usually when wrapping a present, we need "extra" paper to seal off the ends. Estimate how much extra paper is needed for sealing off the ends.

? Hint
See page 156

Think Beyond

c) Wrapping paper is often sold in rolls of 16 square feet. After wrapping the present, how much paper will be left on the roll?

5. Here are the orthogonal views of a rectangular prism. What are the dimensions of the prism? What is its surface area?

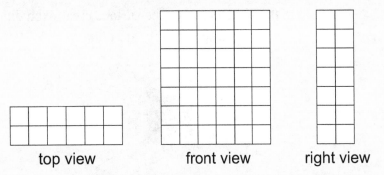

top view   front view   right view

6. Put together a study sheet for your next quiz on surface area by answering the following questions:

a) What is surface area?

b) What units do you use to measure surface area?

c) How can you use the dimensions of a rectangular prism to find its surface area?

d) What formulas can be used to find the surface area of a rectangular prism?

7. Imagine painting the walls, ceiling and floor of the inside of a garage. The garage is 25 ft. wide by 40 ft. long by 10 ft. high.

a) Sketch the orthogonal views of this prism.

b) Find the surface area inside the garage, including the inside of the garage door.

c) A gallon of paint covers 400 ft.^{2} How many gallons will you need to paint all the surfaces in the garage if you plan to use two coats of paint?

 **Hint**
See page 156

8. a) Determine the surface area (excluding the bottom) of this cube structure in square units.

b) Can you use orthogonal views of this building to determine its surface area? Why or why not?

Think Beyond

9. A 4-by-4-by-4-cube is built from 1-inch cubes. This big cube is dipped in red paint and then broken apart into 1-inch cubes again.

a) How many of the 1-inch cubes have three painted faces? How many 1-inch cubes have two painted faces? One painted face? No painted faces?

b) Answer these same questions for an 18-by-18-by-18-inch cube.

c) In an n-by-n-by-n-inch cube, how many of the 1-inch cubes would have three painted faces? How many unit cubes would have two painted faces? One painted face? Zero painted faces?

Think Beyond

10. The surface area of a cube is 216 cm². What are the dimensions of the cube?

11. Write each fraction as a decimal and as a simplified fraction.

    a) $\frac{24}{21}$

    b) $\frac{21}{24}$

12. Find the sum or difference. Show your work.

    a) $\frac{4}{9} + \frac{4}{15}$

    b) $\frac{7}{12} - \frac{12}{3}$

13. Determine the value of x.

    a) $-4x + 7 = -15$

    b) $\frac{x}{9} = -\frac{4}{15}$

14. a) Examine this multiplication pattern: 3, 9, 27, 81.
       If this multiplication pattern continues, identify the 5th, 6th
       and 7th terms.

    b) Write a recursive rule and an explicit rule for this pattern and
       determine the tenth term.

    c) What pattern occurs in the ones digit of the terms in the sequence?
       Why does this pattern occur?

    d) Predict the ones digit of the 100th term.

15. Lex showed his work in simplifying the expression below. Describe
    all of Lex's mistakes and correct them.

    $9 - (3) \cdot 12 \div 9 + 9$

    $= 6 \cdot 12 \div 9 + 9$

    $= 72 \div 9 + 9$

    $= 72 \div 18$

    $= 4$

Using Surface Area

Start It Off

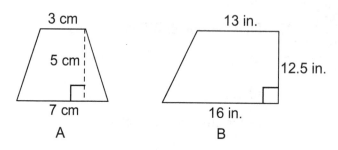

A   B

1. On paper, trace these two trapezoids and draw one diagonal in each.

2. **a)** Find the areas of the two triangles formed by a diagonal in Trapezoid A. Find the area of Trapezoid A.

   b) Find the areas of the two triangles formed by a diagonal in Trapezoid B. Find the area of Trapezoid B.

3. Locate the base of each of the two triangles in each trapezoid. What do you notice? Explain.

4. Explain in words a method for determining the area of a trapezoid.

Using Surface Area

Many everyday projects involve finding the areas of flat surfaces of three-dimensional objects. For example, painting or wallpapering a room, tiling or carpeting a floor, or shingling a roof all involve determining the surface area of space figures.

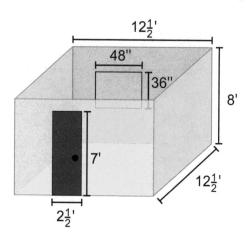

Have you ever painted or wallpapered a room? Juan's older brother just went off to college so Juan is moving into his bedroom. Juan's mother said that if he helps paint the walls and ceiling she will order new carpeting for the floor. Juan is in charge of determining the amount of paint and carpet needed. A drawing of Juan's new bedroom, which is $12\frac{1}{2}$ ft. by $12\frac{1}{2}$ ft. with 8 ft. ceilings, is shown at the left.

Work with a partner to help Juan determine the cost of painting and carpeting his bedroom. You may want to use a calculator.

1. Sketch orthogonal views of the four walls, the ceiling, and the floor. Include windows and doors. Label your sketches.

2. The dimensions of the door in Juan's room is given using feet but the dimensions of the window are given using inches. What do you need to do in order to work efficiently with these measures?

3. Calculate the surface area of the walls and ceiling that will be painted. Don't paint the window or door! Show your work and label all calculations.

4. The room will need two coats of paint everywhere. One gallon of white ceiling paint covers 250 square feet and costs $21.95. One gallon of midnight blue wall paint covers 400 square feet and costs $24.99. What is the cost of the paint for the room?

5. Carpeting is sold by the square yard. If the area of the floor is in square feet, how do you convert this measurement into square yards? Carpet costs $23.49 per square yard. How much will the carpeting for the room cost?

6. What is the total cost of the materials for painting and carpeting Juan's bedroom?

Squares and Square Roots

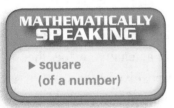

Did you notice that the floor of Juan's room was in the shape of a square? You found that the area of the floor of the bedroom was $\left(12\frac{1}{2}\right)^2$, or $156\frac{1}{4}$ square feet. The square of a number is the product of that number and itself. Squaring a number means multiplying it by itself. The operation of squaring can be indicated by using the exponent 2: $\left(12\frac{1}{2}\right)^2$, 7.3^2, 10^2, and 14^2. You read $\left(12\frac{1}{2}\right)^2$ as "the square of $12\frac{1}{2}$" or "$12\frac{1}{2}$ squared." It may help to visualize this quantity as the area of a square with side length of $12\frac{1}{2}$ units.

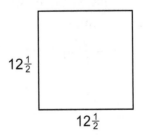

$12\frac{1}{2}$

$12\frac{1}{2}$

Square numbers are positive integers that can be written as the square of some other integer. For example, 16 is a square number since $16 = 4^2$ and 100 is a square number since $100 = 10^2$, but $156\frac{1}{4}$ is not a square number.

7. List the first 12 square numbers.

8. Fractions and decimals can be squared as in the calculation of the area of Juan's room, $\left(12\frac{1}{2}\right)^2$. Mathematicians often use parentheses with fractions, decimals and integers to indicate which part of the number is being squared. What is being squared in each of the examples below?

a) $\left(\frac{2}{5}\right)^2 = \frac{4}{25}$ **c)** $(-1.2)^2 = 1.44$

b) $-1.2^2 = -1.44$ **d)** $-(1.2)^2 = -1.44$

9. Evaluate these expressions.

a) 0.09^2

b) $-\left(2\frac{3}{8}\right)^2$

c) -1.1^2

d) $(-2.5)^2$

e) $\left(4\frac{1}{3}\right)^2$

f) $\left(\frac{-7}{100}\right)^2$

The operation that undoes the squaring of non-negative numbers is the square root. If Juan wanted to build a square closet in his bedroom with an area of 25 square feet, he would need to determine the length of the sides of the closet. He could do this by finding the square root of 25. Juan might think: "What number multiplied by itself equals 25?" There are two possibilities: 5 and -5. Since the length cannot have a negative value, the answer is 5. Mathematicians have a symbol for the positive square root of a number, $\sqrt{n}$ or, in this example, $\sqrt{25}$. They say, "5 is the positive square root of 25, although -5 is another square root of 25."

The relationship between square and square root can be summarized using symbols:

$$5^2 = 25 \text{ and } \sqrt{25} = 5 \text{ or } n \times n = n^2 \text{ and } \sqrt{n^2} = \sqrt{n}.$$

By knowing the first twelve square numbers ($1^2 = 1$, $2^2 = 4$, $3^2 = 9$, $4^2 = 16$, $5^2 = 25$, $6^2 = 36$, $7^2 = 49$, $8^2 = 64$, $9^2 = 81$, $10^2 = 100$, $11^2 = 121$, and $12^2 = 144$), you can approximate the value of a square root. For example, you know that $\sqrt{67.8}$ is between 8 and 9 since $8^2 = 64$ and $9^2 = 81$. A more refined approximation is that the square root is between 8 and 8.5 since 67.8 is closer to 64 than to 81. Using a calculator, $\sqrt{67.8} \approx 8.23$. Most of the time simplifying a square root results in an approximate value rather than an exact value.

10. Find the square roots. Round to the nearest tenths place when appropriate. Do not use the square root key on a calculator.

   a) $\sqrt{89}$

   b) $\sqrt{24}$

   c) $\sqrt{135}$

   d) $\sqrt{400}$

   e) $\sqrt{-1}$

   f) $\sqrt{7 \cdot 7}$

   g) $\sqrt{m^2}$

   h) $\sqrt{\dfrac{16}{25}}$

   i) $\sqrt{55}$

   j) $\sqrt{0.36}$

11. Locate the square root key on your calculator. Use it to find the side length of a square that has an area of 39.0625 square feet. Record the side length in feet and in inches.

Wrap It Up

Explain the key ideas regarding squares and square roots. For example, what is the square of a number? What is the square root of a number? How are squares and square roots related? Discuss how you can approximate the value of a square root.

MATHEMATICALLY
SPEAKING

▶ square (of a number)

▶ square number

▶ square root

Write
About It

1. When finding surface area, there are many things you must consider, such as the shape and dimensions of the surfaces, whether the measurements are fractions or decimals, and how to convert between units (square feet to square yards, inches to feet, and so on). Give advice to Juan on how to make sense of all of these considerations.

2. When Juan goes to the store he finds three different wall paints that he prefers to midnight blue.

   • Daredevil red: $32.99 per gallon; 1 gallon covers approximately 400 ft.^{2}

   • Lime green: $25.85 per gallon; 1 gallon covers approximately 350 ft.^{2}

   • Onyx crystal: $28.98 per gallon; 1 gallon covers approximately 150 ft.^{2}

   Choose a wall color for Juan's room and calculate the cost of two coats of paint.

3. The inside of the Olympic-size swimming pool at the YMCA needs painting. The pool is pictured below. What is the total surface area that needs to be painted?

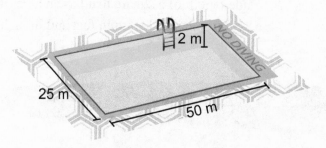

4. Each dimension of the beginner pool at the YMCA is half the corresponding dimension on the Olympic-size pool described in Question 3. This pool also needs to be painted.

   a) Determine the surface area that needs to be painted.

   b) If a liter of paint covers 8.6 square meters, how many liters will you need to paint the beginner pool?

5. The city of Irvine, California boasts that it has a junior-Olympic pool. The pool is 75 feet long and 5 feet deep, and each of the six lanes is 7 feet wide. In addition, the two outside lanes are an extra 1.5 feet wide.

   a) Sketch the pool.

   b) What is the width of the pool?

   c) Determine the interior surface area of the pool.

   d) Show your steps for finding the surface area.

6. Hurricanes can cause tremendous damage to roofs. The building in the picture lost its roof when a hurricane hit Florida. New asphalt shingles cost $0.80 per square foot. In order to have enough shingles, builders always increase the square footage of a roof by 10% and use that area in their calculations for the cost of shingles.

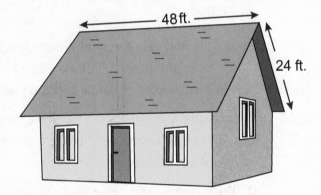

   a) Imagine that you are a builder. Estimate the area of the roof for the house.

   b) Calculate the actual cost of new asphalt shingles for the roof.

   c) Wind- and impact-resistant shingles are now being sold in certain areas of the country. These specialized shingles cost 50% more than regular asphalt shingles. What is the price if the owners decide to use these wind-resistant shingles?

7. How much cardboard is needed to make this cereal box? Figure an extra 10% of the surface area for the cardboard to make the flaps to seal the box.

26 cm

18.5 cm   5 cm

8. The area of a regulation softball infield (inside the bases) is 3,600 ft.^{2}. The Fay School softball infield was incorrectly built and the infield has an area of 3,422.25 ft.^{2}. If the infield is in the shape of a square, what is the distance between bases on the Fay School softball field?

9. Record the important points you need to remember about the concept of a square root. Use this information when studying.

10. Estimate the following using what you know about square numbers.

a) $\sqrt{8}$

b) $\sqrt{0.64}$

c) $\sqrt{42\frac{1}{4}}$

d) $\sqrt{1,500}$

 Think Beyond

11. Investigate methods for approximating square roots of numbers at `http://mathforum.org/library/drmath/view/61909.html`. In your own words, explain a method you found. Give examples.

 Think Beyond

12. Fire codes in many states now indicate that classrooms cannot have more than 40% of the surface area of the walls covered with teaching materials, wall displays or art.

a) What is the surface area of the walls of your math classroom? Does your classroom meet the fire code?

b) Describe how teachers can estimate whether or not their classroom meets the 40% rule.

13. Write each phrase as an algebraic expression.

   a) twenty-nine subtracted from a number p

   b) the quotient of eleven and r

   c) three times the sum of x and two and five tenths

   d) the product of negative eight and y divided by $y + 1$

14. Determine the greatest common factor (GCF) of

   a) 18, 24 and 30.

   b) 39 and 52.

15. $\frac{7}{6} \div 2\frac{1}{5}$

16. $2\left(\frac{-3}{4} \div \frac{1}{5}\right)$

17. Use the graph below to answer the following questions.

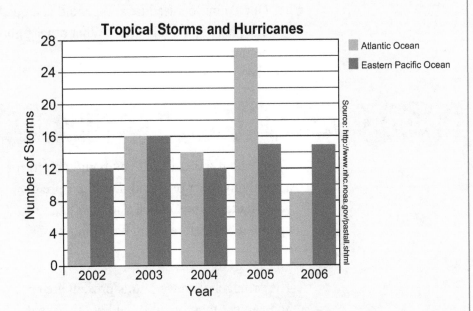

a) From 2002 to 2006, which ocean had the more active tropical storm and hurricane season?

b) What was the average number of storms that occurred each year from 2002−2006 for each ocean?

c) Vince said that it looked like one of the oceans had more than 50% of the total number of tropical storms and hurricanes that are displayed on the graph. Is he correct? Why or why not?

Another Formula for Surface Area

➡️ Start It Off

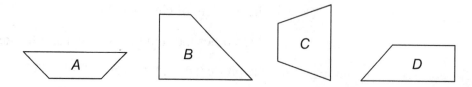

1. Figures A–D are trapezoids. With your partner, make a list of common features of all of the trapezoids. Next, list any differences you notice.

2. You may have observed that figures A and C appear to have two congruent, opposite sides. We call trapezoids with two congruent opposite sides _____ trapezoids.

3. Write a definition of a trapezoid.

4. Mathematicians are not in agreement on how to define a trapezoid. One definition used is: a trapezoid is a quadrilateral having "*at least* one pair of parallel sides." What other figures would fit this alternative definition?

Using the Lateral-Surface Rectangle

Think about the last time you bought a gift for a family member or friend. Did the store give you a flattened box which you then had to fold up into a box before using wrapping paper?

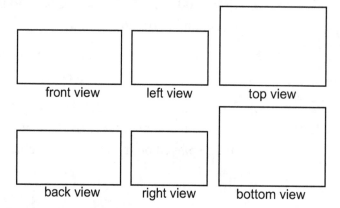

The orthogonal views of this present are shown below. You can put these views together to make the net of the box.

| front view | left view | top view |

| back view | right view | bottom view |

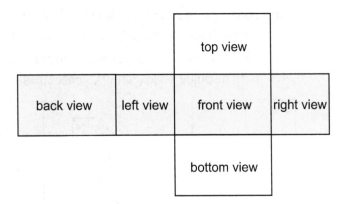

The front, back and side views form the lateral-surface rectangle, which is in green.

Let's Review The lateral-surface rectangle is a rectangle formed by combining the lateral-surfaces of a prism together. The lateral-surface rectangle does not include the bases of the prism.

Below are the nets of two boxes—one is a rectangular prism and the other is a triangular prism.

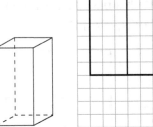
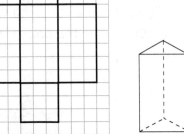
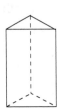
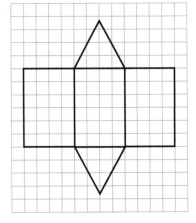

1. Cut out a copy of each net and fold it into a prism. Label the bases and lightly shade the lateral-surface rectangle on each of them.

2. **a)** What is the height of each prism? What is the perimeter of the base of each prism?

   b) What are the dimensions of the lateral-surface rectangle?

   c) How are the measurements in Part a related to the measurements in Part b for both prisms?

3. **a)** Fold a piece of notebook paper into a rectangular prism with a square base (with the base missing). Call it Prism A. Take another piece of notebook paper and fold it into a *different* rectangular prism with a square base (with the base missing). Call it Prism B.

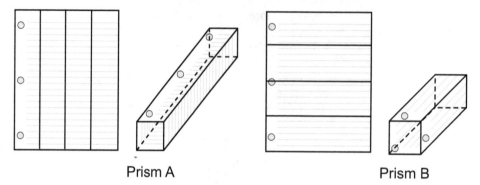

Prism A   Prism B

   b) What is the same about the prisms? What is different?

   c) What is the perimeter of the base of each prism? What are the dimensions of the lateral-surface rectangle of each prism?

4. Imagine that Prism A and B have bases. Without calculating, which prism from Question 3 has the greater surface area? Explain your reasoning.

5. **a)** Now fold a piece of notebook paper into a triangular prism with a base that is an equilateral triangle (with the base missing). Call it Prism C. Take another piece of notebook paper and fold it into a *different* triangular prism with a base that is an equilateral triangle (with the base missing). Call it Prism D.

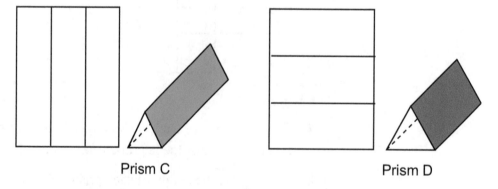

Prism C   Prism D

   b) What is the same about the two prisms? What is different?

   c) How is one of the dimensions of the lateral-surface rectangle related to the perimeter of the base of each prism? What are the dimensions of the lateral-surface rectangle in each prism?

   d) Imagine that Prisms C and D have bases. Without calculating, decide which of the two triangular prisms has the greater surface area. Explain your thinking.

In many Asian and European countries, the surface area of a prism is calculated using the areas of the lateral-surface rectangle and the bases. Let's generalize a formula.

6. a) Find the area of the bases of the prism below on the left.

   b) Find the area of the lateral-surface rectangle for the prism on the left.

   c) Describe in words how to find the surface area of the prism on the left using Parts a and b.

   d) What is the surface area of this prism?

   e) Examine the drawing of the prism on the right. What is the effect of changing the orientation of a prism on the calculations used to determine surface area?

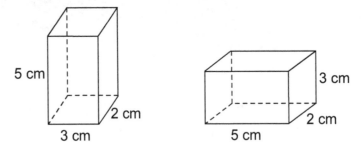

7. a) Write a rule for calculating the surface area of a rectangular prism. Let *SA* represent surface area, *B* represent the area of a base of the prism, *p* represent the perimeter of a base of the prism, *l* represent length, *w* represent width and *h* represent height.

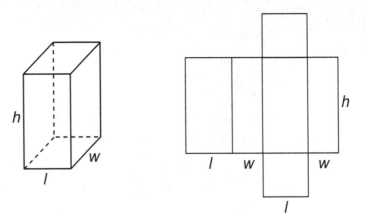

   b) Write a general rule that can be used to find the surface area of all prisms, regardless of the shape of the bases.

Can rectangular prisms hold the same amount but have different surface areas? Below are five boxes that each hold 36 cubic centimeters.

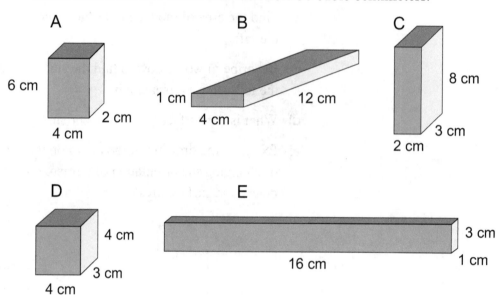

A   6 cm   2 cm   4 cm

B   1 cm   12 cm   4 cm

C   8 cm   3 cm   2 cm

D   4 cm   3 cm   4 cm

E   3 cm   16 cm   1 cm

8. Determine the surface area of each box. Which box has the least surface area? Which box has the greatest surface area?

9. Zoe stated, "The shape of a box determines whether its surface area will be large or small." What do you think Zoe means by this statement?

Wrap It Up

Explain how to find the surface area of a triangular prism using the lateral-surface rectangle and bases. Use the example below.

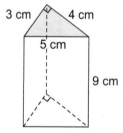

3 cm   4 cm
5 cm
9 cm

Write About It

1. Explain the different parts of the formula for the surface area of a prism: $SA = 2B + perimeter\ of\ base \bullet h$, where SA represents surface area, B represents the area of each base, and h represents height. Demonstrate how the formula works by finding the surface area of a prism that you choose.

2. Measure this prism in centimeters and then determine its surface area.

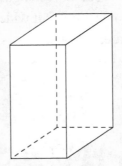

For each of the following prisms, determine the surface area. Show your steps.

3.

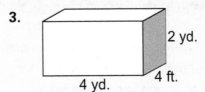

2 yd.
4 ft.
4 yd.

4.

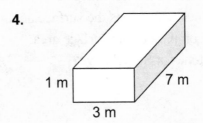

1 m
3 m
7 m

5.

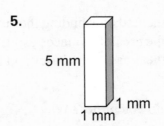

5 mm
1 mm
1 mm

6. Imagine folding this net into a cube. Which letters are on faces opposite each other? Build the cube to check.

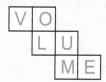

7. Stonehenge in England is an ancient site consisting of huge slabs of stone. Many are in the shape of rectangular prisms. The largest stones weigh over 20 tons! Some are 8 feet wide, 5 feet thick, and 25 feet tall. Calculate the surface area of these stones.

8. Other ancient cultures also built monuments in the shape of rectangular prisms. The Maya built "stelae" to commemorate important events. One stelae is 35 feet tall, 5 feet wide and $4\frac{1}{4}$ feet thick. How does the surface area of this stone compare to the surface area of the large stones at Stonehenge?

9. You now have two methods for finding the surface area of a prism—finding the sum of the area of the faces using orthogonal views, and finding the sum of the areas of the bases and the area of the lateral-surfaces using nets.

    a) Which method do you prefer? Why?

    b) Why are these two methods equivalent? Explain with words and with symbols.

Find the surface area of the prisms in Questions 10–12 below. You may wish to sketch the nets.

10.

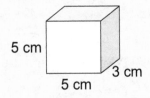

5 cm

5 cm

3 cm

11.

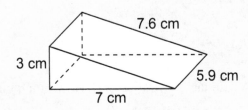

7.6 cm

3 cm

5.9 cm

7 cm

12.

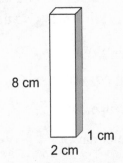

8 cm

1 cm

2 cm

13. The Matthews just got a new 32-inch flat-screen TV. The box that it comes in has a surface area of $28\frac{3}{4}$ square feet. The base is 3 feet by $1\frac{1}{4}$ feet. What is the height of the box that holds the new TV?

14. Fancy soap is sometimes packaged in a box in the shape of a triangular prism. The triangular bases are equilateral triangles.

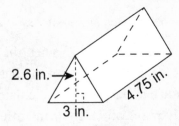

2.6 in.

3 in.

4.75 in.

a) What is the surface area of the box?

b) Draw the net of this prism and fold the net to "build" the prism.

Think
Beyond

15. Find the surface area of this regular hexagonal prism.

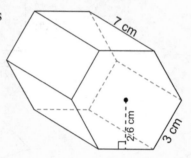

7 cm

2.6 cm

3 cm

Think
Back

16. A sale tag says "40% off." How much will you save on a pair of jeans that are $60.00?

17. You have studied two scales for measuring temperature. What are they called? For both scales give the temperature of

   a) the boiling point of water.

   b) the freezing point of water.

   c) average room temperature.

   d) a very hot summer day.

18. On the coordinate plane, which of the following is true of all the points that fall on the x-axis?

   A. All the coordinates are negative.

   B. The y-coordinate is zero.

   C. The x-coordinate is zero.

   D. All the x-coordinates are positive.

19. School Suppliers, Inc. offers 15 scientific calculators for $412.50. Calculators R Us, a major competitor, has a deal for the same calculators. You can purchase 25 calculators from Calculators R Us for $650.00. Explain which company offers the better deal.

20. **True or False**

   Equilateral triangles are the only triangles that have any congruent sides. Kathy circled **True**. Why is her answer wrong?

Volume

Start It Off

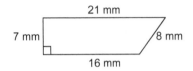

21 mm

7 mm

8 mm

16 mm

1. Copy the trapezoid and draw in one diagonal to form two triangles. Label the base of one triangle "b_1" and the base of the other triangle "b_2." Label the height h. Use b_1, b_2 and h, and write a formula for the area of each triangle and the area of the trapezoid.

2. Find the area of the trapezoid.

3. Using the distributive property of multiplication over addition, rewrite the formula.

4. Some students use $A = \frac{1}{2}(b_1 + b_2)h$ to find the area of a trapezoid, while other students use $A = \frac{1}{2}h(b_1 + b_2)$. Are these formulas equivalent to $A = \frac{1}{2}b_1h + \frac{1}{2}b_2h$? Explain your reasoning using words and symbols.

MATHEMATICALLY SPEAKING

▸ Volume

Let's Review

Volume is the amount of space contained in a three-dimensional solid. The volume of a solid is measured using cubic units such as cubic centimeters, cubic meters, and cubic inches. Cubic units are abbreviated by raising the unit to the third power (unit^3, cm^3, m3, in^3).

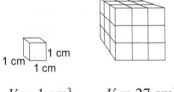

1 cm

1 cm

1 cm

$V = 1 \text{ cm}^3$ $\qquad V = 27 \text{ cm}^3$

To develop the formula for the volume of a rectangular prism, imagine building a base that is 1 unit high and finding the volume of the base. One way to find the volume of the base is by counting the number of cubes. A more efficient way to find the number of cubes in the base is to multiply the length of the base by the width of the base. In the diagram on the next page, the base is 4 units by 7 units and has an area of 28 units^2. Since the base is 1 unit high, it has a volume of 28 units^3.

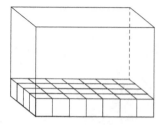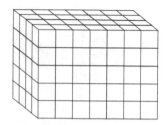

To build this rectangular prism, you continue to add layers of 28 cubes. The rectangular prism above on the right has 5 layers. The volume of this rectangular prism can be determined by multiplying the length by the width by the height of the prism. Volume of this prism can also be found by multiplying the area of the base by the height of the prism.

$$V = lwh \qquad\qquad V = Area_{base} \times h$$

Generalizing Volume Formulas

The idea of stacking can also be used to determine the volume of other prisms. Have you ever tasted Swiss chocolate, Toblerone®? It comes in a box in the shape of a triangular prism.

In the drawing above, notice how there are layers of triangles in the box. If you turn the box, the layers will be stacked vertically, and the height of the stack will be the height of the triangular prism. Containers for Kids is hoping to make boxes in the shape of triangular prisms and fill them with crackers. Hence, the company needs to be able to calculate the volume of different types of prisms.

1. Take a stack of green pattern blocks and build a model of the Toblerone® chocolate bar. What measurements do you need to determine the volume of the box?

2. Write a formula for finding the volume of the box. Why can't you use the formula $V = l \cdot w \cdot h$? Can you use the formula $V = B \cdot h$ where B represents the area of the base of the prism? Explain.

3. Bars of Toblerone® come in different sizes but the most common one is shown below. Calculate the volume of this triangular prism with equilateral triangles as bases. Record your steps.

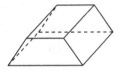

20.8 cm

3.1 cm

3.6 cm

Use the red trapezoid pattern blocks and make a prism with bases in the shape of trapezoids. This prism is called a trapezoidal prism. Make it 6 layers high or rotate the prism so it is 6 layers deep.

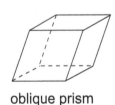

4. Write a formula that can be used to calculate the volume of this trapezoidal prism. Consider other formulas you know and use the idea of layers to generate the formula.

5. Measure the red trapezoid pattern block in centimeters. Find the actual volume of the prism you constructed.

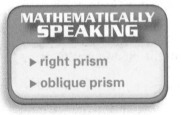

MATHEMATICALLY SPEAKING

▶ **right prism**
▶ **oblique prism**

The prisms studied so far have all been right prisms as the edges are perpendicular to the base, and the bases are aligned directly over each other. All of the lateral-surfaces of right prisms are rectangles. Imagine taking a cube made out of JELL-O® and pushing on the top base so that it becomes what is known as an oblique prism. The bases of oblique prisms are not aligned on top of each other and the lateral-surfaces are all parallelograms instead of rectangles.

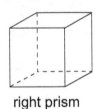

right prism   oblique prism

6. You use the same volume formula for oblique prisms, $V = B \cdot h$, since you can still imagine making stacks of the base polygon. Determine the volume of the prism below.

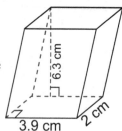

6.3 cm
3.9 cm
2 cm

Capacity

We often use the term *capacity* to refer to volume. Capacity is the greatest volume that a container can hold. Think of a prism that can be filled, such as a milk container, and a prism that cannot be filled, such as a solid brick. We can measure the volume of both objects, but we can only measure the capacity of the milk container.

Usually we use the term *capacity* when we are describing how much a container can hold. To measure capacity, we can use cubic units or we can use units such as cups and gallons, in the customary system, and liters and milliliters in the metric system. When you found how much chocolate fits inside a box, you were calculating the capacity of the box. In that case, you measured capacity in cubic units.

7. a) List some units used to indicate capacity in the customary system.

  b) Examine the pictures below. Notice that the capacity of each bottle or container is given in the U.S. customary units and in metric units. Give both measures for each container.

1 cup (237 mL)

Apple Juice
NATURAL
100%
12 fl oz
(355 mL)

1 pint 7.7 fl oz
(700 mL)

MILK

half gallon (1.89 L)

8. a) What is the relationship between liters and milliliters?

  b) What are the abbreviations for liters and milliliters?

  c) List some common items that are sold in 1- or 2-liter containers.

In the metric system, the units used to measure volume and capacity are related. A cube with a length, width and height of 1 centimeter has a volume of 1 cubic centimeter (1 cm³). A cube with a volume of 1 cubic centimeter has capacity of 1 milliliter (1 mL).

$1 \text{ cm}^3 = 1 \text{ mL}$

A milliliter is a very small amount of liquid. It is about $\frac{1}{5}$ of a teaspoon.

1 cm
1 cm
1 cm

Since 1 cm³ = 1 mL, then 1000 cm³ = 1000 mL = 1 liter. The relationship between cubic centimeters and milliliters makes recording capacity and volume easy in the metric system. A 3 × 2 × 6 cm rectangular prism has a volume of 36 cm³. If you filled this same prism with liquid, you could record its capacity as 36 mL as well as 36 cm³.

9. **a)** Juice boxes are often in the shape of rectangular prisms. The dimensions of one box are approximately 6.5 cm by 3.5 cm by 10 cm. What is the volume of this juice box?

    b) Find the capacity of the juice box. Record the amount of apple juice in the box in milliliters.

    c) Record the capacity of the juice box in liters.

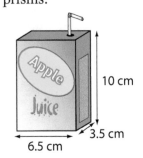

Apple Juice

10 cm

3.5 cm

6.5 cm

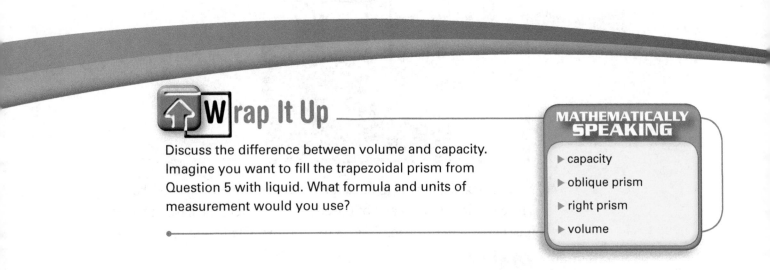

Wrap It Up

Discuss the difference between volume and capacity. Imagine you want to fill the trapezoidal prism from Question 5 with liquid. What formula and units of measurement would you use?

MATHEMATICALLY SPEAKING

▶ capacity

▶ oblique prism

▶ right prism

▶ volume

Write
About It

1. Explain to a friend the relationship between volume and capacity.

2. In art class, students at the Abigail Adams Middle School built 3-D structures out of straws. One structure turned out to be quite unsteady.

   a) What type of prism did the students build?

   b) What is the volume of this prism?

   c) How might students stabilize their structure?

3. The Cheese Shop has a huge model of a wedge of Swiss cheese in the shape of a triangular prism outside their store. The triangular base of the prism has a base length of 1 yd and a height of $7\frac{1}{4}$ ft. The Swiss cheese wedge is $4\frac{3}{4}$ ft. tall. What is the volume of the triangular prism?

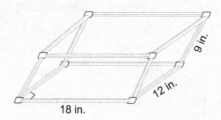

4. Milk is boxed and sold in rectangular prisms in many parts of the world. The capacity of one brand of boxed milk is 1 liter. The base of the box measures 9 cm by 6 cm. What is the approximate height of the box?

Hint
See page 156

5. Many kindergarten classrooms have a water table so children can learn about the capacity of containers. One table is $1\frac{1}{2}$ meters long, 1 meter wide and 40 centimeters deep. What is the volume of the water table in cubic centimeters? In liters?

6. This fish tank is 16 inches long, $7\frac{1}{2}$ inches wide and $14\frac{1}{2}$ inches high.

a) What is the volume of the tank?

b) Pet stores in the United States describe fish tanks by their capacity— that is, by the number of gallons they hold. How many cups are in a gallon? How many quarts are in a gallon? Why is the relationship between capacity and volume so much easier to remember in the metric system?

c) If there are approximately 231 cubic inches in every gallon, how many gallons of water will the tank hold?

7. a) If 25 of the trapezoidal prisms shown at right were stacked, determine the volume of the large trapezoidal prism they would create.

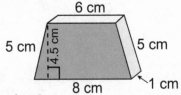

b) What is the surface area of the large prism?

8. Boxes of different sizes in the shape of right triangular prisms similar to the one at right are needed to package cheese wedges. Use the drawing and dimensions in the table to answer Questions 8–10.

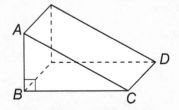

Copy and complete the table.

	AB	BC	CD	Area of ABC	Volume of Prism
a)	8 cm	15 cm	6 cm		
b)		8 cm	12 cm	12 cm²	
c)	12 cm		9 cm		270 cm³

Think Beyond

9. Add a column to the table in Question 8 labeled "Surface Area," and determine the amount of cardboard needed for each box.

10. Imagine that the boxes in Question 8 are made of plastic and filled with juice. What are the capacities of each triangular prism in milliliters and in liters?

11. Loose tea is often stored in rectangular tins. One tin is 8 cm by 6 cm by 12 cm, but it is only three-fourths full. How much tea is in this container?

12. Find the volume of the following prisms. Record your work.

a)
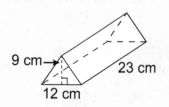
9 cm
23 cm
12 cm

b)
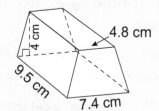
4 cm
4.8 cm
9.5 cm
7.4 cm

c)
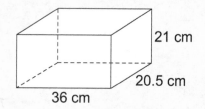
21 cm
20.5 cm
36 cm

13. The $5\frac{1}{2}$ liters of oil drained from an SUV filled a rectangular container that has a square base with sides 15 cm long. What is the depth of the oil in the container?

Think Beyond

14 a) An open rectangular box for storing office supplies has walls and a base that are 2 cm thick and interior dimensions of 30 cm long by 24 cm wide by 6 cm deep. What are the exterior dimensions of the box?

b) What is the capacity of this box?

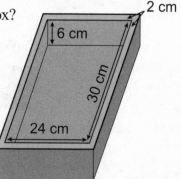
2 cm
6 cm
30 cm
24 cm

c) What is the exterior surface area of the box?

d) How much wood was needed to build it?

15. A Boeing 747 can travel at a cruising speed of about 550 miles per hour. What is the approximate flying time for a flight from Cleveland to Houston if the two cities are about 1,300 miles apart? Give your answer in hours and minutes.

16. What is the difference between an expression and an equation? Give examples of both.

17. **a)** Active Life, your favorite sporting goods store, is going out of business. The store is advertising 60% off all items. You decide to buy two pairs of sneakers that normally cost $79.99 per pair. What is the sale price for two pairs of sneakers?

    b) If you have to pay 10% sales tax on the sale price, what is the total cost for the sneakers?

18. Place these fractions in order from least to greatest using the symbols $<, =$ or $>$.

    a) $\dfrac{1}{13}, \dfrac{1}{10}, \dfrac{1}{11}$

    b) $-\dfrac{7}{10}, -\dfrac{7}{6}, -\dfrac{7}{8}$

19. Is the value of this expression positive or negative: $\dfrac{(-4)(-5)(-6)}{(-2)} \cdot \dfrac{1}{-4}$? Explain how you know without calculating.

Scale Models

➡ Start It Off

Jaclyn remembers the formula for the area of a trapezoid by thinking of the formula for a parallelogram. She makes two copies of the trapezoid, flips one of them and slides the trapezoids together to form the parallelogram.

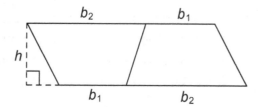

1. Draw or trace two identical trapezoids and follow the directions above to make a parallelogram. Use h, b_1 and b_2 to label the parallelogram.

2. What is the area of the parallelogram above? Using the formula for the parallelogram, what is the area of each trapezoid?

3. Lee thinks the formulas $A = \frac{1}{2}(b_1 + b_2)h$ and $A = \frac{(b_1 + b_2)h}{2}$ are different. Claire thinks they are the same. Who do you agree with and why?

4. You now have two ways to explain the formula for area of a trapezoid using either triangles or a parallelogram. Describe the approach that makes the most sense to you and that you will remember.

Miniatures have always appealed to people. Have you ever seen a model train set complete with a tiny village and conductors? Or have you built miniature castles or rocket ships out of interlocking blocks?

Building Miniature Boxes

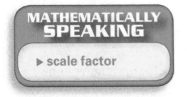
Containers for Kids knows that miniature boxes will be very appealing to kids and wants to produce lots of different miniatures. But how do you create a miniature? Let's use a cereal box as an example. The dimensions of one box are 7 inches by 3 inches by 12 inches. You can make a miniature by multiplying each dimension of the box by a number that is less than 1, such as $\frac{1}{2}$, $\frac{1}{4}$ or $\frac{2}{5}$. You must multiply each dimension by the same number. This number is called the scale factor. Scale factors are used to make scale models.

Containers for Kids decides to experiment with a scale factor of $\frac{1}{2}$.

1. What is the effect of multiplying any number by a number that is less than 1?

2. Using the scale factor $\frac{1}{2}$, determine the dimensions of your miniature.

3. Draw the net of your miniature box. You may want to add a tab to the end of the lateral-surface rectangle and to one of the bases so you can tape the faces together.

You can make your miniature look realistic by either drawing details on the faces of the net or by using a photocopy machine to make a reduction of the faces of the box. Since the scale factor is $\frac{1}{2}$, you need to reduce the images by 50%. Glue these images onto the faces of your box. When you fold it up, you will have a miniature!

4. a) Find the surface area and volume of the original cereal box.

   b) Find the surface area and volume of your miniature.

5. a) How many times the miniature's surface area is the original's surface area?

b) How many times the miniature's volume is the original volume?

6. a) Explain why the surface area of the miniature is not half the surface area of the original cereal box.

b) What is the relationship between the scale factor and the surface area of the miniature?

7. a) Explain why the volume of the miniature is not half the volume of the original cereal box.

b) What is the relationship between the scale factor and the volume of the miniature?

8. Containers for Kids decides it needs to make even smaller boxes! Make another miniature box using a scale factor of $\frac{1}{3}$ or $\frac{1}{6}$. Decorate your box to appeal to kids.

rap It Up

Describe the relationships you discovered in this lesson regarding scale factors, surface area and volume.

MATHEMATICALLY SPEAKING

▶ scale factor

MATERIALS LIST

▶ Calculator
▶ Ruler

Write
About It

1. When you make a miniature of a prism, the dimensions are reduced by a scale factor. To create a miniature, the scale factors will be less than _____. To make an enlarged prism, the scale factor will be greater than $\frac{1}{2}$ _____. Give directions on how to make a miniature box.

2. a) What scale factor would you use to make a miniature of a shoe box if the original dimensions are 15 in. by 8 in. by 5 in.? Give the dimensions of the miniature box.

   b) How many times the surface area of the original shoe box would the surface area of the miniature shoe box be?

3. Cindy examined the net of the prism below and stated, "The volume of this prism is 62 cubic units." Is she correct? Explain.

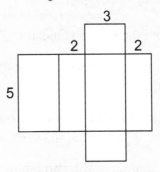

4. I'm thinking of a cube that has a volume of 27 cubic yards. What is the surface area of this cube?

5. Ken wants to make a giant model of a tent for a school play. A regular tent is shown. It has equilateral triangles as bases. Use a scale factor of 4 and give the dimensions of the enlarged prism. How much fabric in square yards will it take to make this big model?

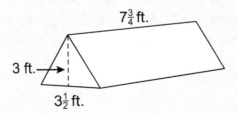

6. Lela stated, "Square centimeters, cubic centimeters, regular centimeters—I can't keep them straight." Give Lela some advice on how to make sense of these different measures.

7. Imagine that you have 24 1-centimeter cubes to arrange into the shape of a rectangular prism. List the dimensions for six different prisms that can be made using all 24 cubes. Copy the table and record your results.

	Length	Width	Height	Volume
a)				24 cm³
b)				24 cm³
c)				24 cm³
d)				24 cm³
e)				24 cm³
f)				24 cm³

8. Use the data from the table in Question 7.

   a) What are the dimensions of the prism with the greatest surface area? The least surface area?

   b) Take the prism with the greatest surface area and reduce it using a scale factor of $\frac{1}{4}$. What is the surface area of the reduction?

   c) What is the volume of this miniature?

9. Tissues comes in many differently shaped rectangular boxes. One box is 22 cm by 12 cm by 5 cm. Another box is 11 cm by 11 cm by 11 cm.

   a) Which box has the greatest capacity?

   b) Which box takes the least amount of cardboard to make? Assume there are no overlaps.

   c) The cubic box of tissues costs $2.15, and the rectangular prism box costs $2.71. Assume both boxes are filled to the top with the same thickness of tissues. Which is the better buy? Explain.

10. Rubik's Cube™ puzzles have been challenging students since the 1980s. Each face of a solved Rubik's Cube™ consists of nine small squares of one color. If each small square has a side length of $\frac{3}{4}$ inch, what is the surface area of the cube?

11. Draw a net that could be used to make a miniature Rubik's Cube™. Fold the net into a cube.

12. What is the volume of your miniature Rubik's Cube™?

13. Imagine enlarging the cereal box on page 129 by a scale factor of 20. What would the enlarged box look like? How would the surface area and the volume of this enlargement compare to the original measures?

 Think Beyond

14. What is the surface area of a cube with the following volume:

a) 3,000 m³

b) 1,728 cm³

c) If you enlarged the cube in Part b using a scale factor of 2.5, what would be the surface area and volume of the enlargement?

 Think Beyond

15. Perfect cubes are the cubes of positive integers (that is, positive integers raised to the third power). What patterns do you notice in the prime factorization of perfect cubes that are odd numbers (for example, 27 and 125)? What patterns do you notice in the prime factorization of perfect cubes that are even numbers (for example, 8 and 64)?

**Think
Back**

16. Express each situation as an expression or an equation.

    a) Sharon ran five-sixths as many miles as Harold.

    b) Sixty minutes is equal to twice the amount of time Jen needed to finish the quiz.

17. Solve these equations. Show all steps.

    a) $-3m + 1 = -26$

    b) $2k + \dfrac{7}{4} = \dfrac{9}{16}$

18. Estimate the answer: $93 \cdot (0.512)$. Explain your thinking.

19. Show your work: $9.16008 \div 0.24$.

20. What is a ratio? Explain using words, pictures and symbols.

Optional Technology Lesson
for this section available
in your eBook

Sum It Up

Surface Area of Rectangular Prisms

The surface area of a three-dimensional shape is the area of the outside of the figure. One method to find the surface area of a rectangular prism is to use orthogonal views and find the surface area of the different faces.

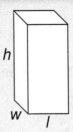

This rectangular prism has three different faces.

$SA_{\text{rectangular prism}} = 2lw + 2lh + 2wh$ or

$SA_{\text{rectangular prism}} = 2(lw + lh + wh)$

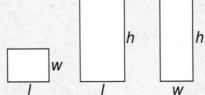

Another way to determine the surface area of a rectangular prism is to sum the areas of the bases and the lateral-surface rectangle. Sometimes the net of the figure helps you visualize the lateral-surface.

$SA_{\text{prism}} = area\ of\ bases + lateral\text{-}surface\ rectangle\ area$

$SA_{\text{prism}} = 2 \bullet area\ of\ base + perimeter\ of\ base \bullet height\ of\ prism$

$SA_{\text{prism}} = 2lw + h(l + w + l + w)$

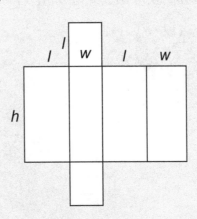

The formula for the area of the bases and the lateral-surface rectangle can be generalized to all prisms. To find the surface area of other types of prisms you also can add the areas of the individual faces.

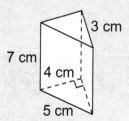

This triangular prism that has four different faces.

$SA_{tri\ prism}$ = 2 • (*area of triangular base*) + *areas of rectangular faces*

$SA_{tri\ prism}$ = $2 \cdot \left(\left(\frac{1}{2}\right) \cdot 4 \cdot 3\right) + (7 \cdot 5) + (7 \cdot 4) + (7 \cdot 3)$

$SA_{tri\ prism}$ = 12 + 35 + 28 + 21

$SA_{tri\ prism}$ = 96 cm²

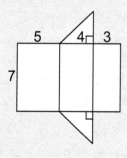

$SA_{tri\ prism}$ = *area of bases + area of lateral-surface rectangle*

$SA_{tri\ prism}$ = $2 \cdot \left(\frac{1}{2}bh\right) +$ *perimeter of triangular base • height of prism*

$SA_{tri\ prism}$ = $2 \cdot \left(\frac{1}{2} \cdot 4 \cdot 3\right) + (12 \cdot 7)$

$SA_{tri\ prism}$ = 12 + 84

$SA_{tri\ prism}$ = 96 cm²

Volume of Prisms

The volume of a prism is the amount of material that fills the prism. Volume is also defined as the amount of space the prism occupies. Capacity is the greatest volume a container can hold. We measure volume using cubic units and capacity using cubic units, milliliters, liters and kiloliters.

To develop the formula for the volume of a prism, imagine building a base that is 1 unit high and finding the area of the base. Add more and more layers, one on top of another, until you reach the height of the prism.

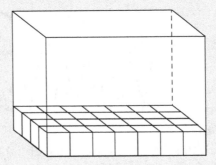 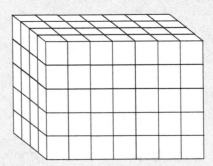

So, to calculate the volume of a prism, multiply the area of the base of the prism by the height.

$V_{prism} = Bh$, where B is the area of the base of the prism.

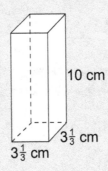

10 cm

$3\frac{1}{3}$ cm

$3\frac{1}{3}$ cm

$$V_{prism} = Bh$$
$$V_{prism} = \left(3\frac{1}{3} \cdot 3\frac{1}{3}\right) \cdot 10$$
$$V_{prism} = \left(\frac{100}{9}\right) \cdot 10$$
$$V_{prism} = \frac{1000}{9} \text{ or } 111\frac{1}{9} \text{ cm}^3$$

Circles

- The circumference of a circle is the distance around the circle. The formulas for circumference C where d is the diameter and r is the radius are:

$$C = 2\pi r \quad C = \pi d$$

- The area of a circle can be found by cutting a circle into wedges and arranging them to form a parallelogram.

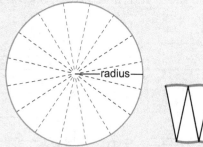 

The base of the parallelogram is half the circumference of the circle, or $\frac{1}{2}(2\pi r)$. The height of the parallelogram is the radius of the circle. The area of the circle is given by:

$$Area_{circle} = \frac{1}{2}(2\pi r) \cdot r$$
$$= \pi r^2$$

MATHEMATICALLY SPEAKING

Do you know what these mathematical terms mean?

▸ capacity	▸ diameter	▸ scale factor
▸ center	▸ irrational number	▸ square (of a number)
▸ chord	▸ oblique prism	▸ square number
▸ circle	▸ pi (π)	▸ square root
▸ circumference	▸ radius (radii)	▸ surface area
▸ concentric	▸ right prism	▸ volume

Part 1. What did you learn?

1. Tropical Fish just installed a new all-glass saltwater fish tank in their San Francisco store. It is 5 feet long by 18 inches wide by 3 feet high.

   a. How much glass was used in building this giant tank?

   b. How much water does this tank hold?

   c. One cubic foot of water weighs approximately 62.4 pounds. The store is planning to install the tank on a table that will hold 1,000 pounds. Will the table be able to support the tank? Explain.

2. Cerin, the daughter of the owner of Tropical Fish, wants a similar fish tank for her bedroom. However, it will have to be a miniature version of the store tank, using a scale factor of $\frac{1}{2}$.

   a. How much glass is needed to build Cerin's tank?

   b. How much water will her tank hold?

   c. Discuss how you found the solutions to Parts a and b and how they're related to the original tank.

3. Find the surface area of the rectangular prism whose net is pictured below using two different methods. Show your work.

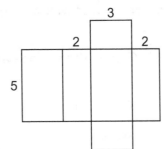

Measurements given in units.
Figure not drawn to scale.

4. Explain to a seventh grader how to find the volume and surface area of a right triangular prism. Use diagrams, words and formulas.

5. Daniel works at a bakery and made a large cake for Tropical Fish's grand re-opening. The cake measured 1 meter by 1.75 meters by 0.5 meters.

   a. Describe the difference between volume and capacity. Would you find the volume or the capacity of the cake? Why?

   b. Find the volume or capacity in both cubic centimeters and cubic meters or milliliters and liters. Explain how you converted between the two measures.

6. Write about the difference between the units used to measure surface area and the units used to measure volume.

7. Find the area of the shape below. Use 3.14 for π. Round your answer to the nearest tenth of a centimeter.

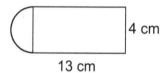

4 cm

13 cm

Part 2. What went wrong?

8. Penelope chose answer B for the multiple choice question below, but her answer was marked wrong. What can you do or say to help Penelope understand why her answer was wrong and how to get the right answer?

   A cube has a volume of 512 cm³. What is the surface area of the cube?

   A. 8 cm²   **C.** 64 cm²

   B. 256 cm²   **D.** 384 cm²

9. Jorge was asked to find the surface area of the rectangular prism pictured below.

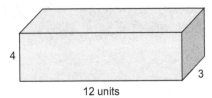

12 units

This is Jorge's explanation of what he did:

"I found 12(3) = 36 for the base. There are two bases so 36 + 36 = 72. Then I found the area of the lateral-surface rectangle by multiplying 12 by 4 so the area of the box is 72 + 48 = 120 units."

Find and correct the error(s) in Jorge's reasoning. Then, find the true surface area of the box. What would you say to Jorge to help him realize his mistake(s)?

10. Rosario was asked to find the perimeter of the shape below.

Here is her work:

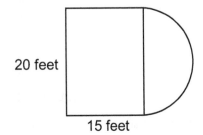

20 feet

15 feet

Semicircle:
$C = \pi 2r$
$C = \pi 2(20)$
$C = 40\pi$
$\frac{1}{2}C = 20\pi$

Rectangle:
$P = 2l + 2w$
$P = 2(20) + 2(15)$
$P = 70$

The perimeter of the figure is $70 + 20\pi$ or approximately 133 inches.

Rosario made two errors in her calculations. Identify each error and then find the correct perimeter of the figure.

Unit Study Guide

Sizing Up Solids: **Focusing on Angles, Surface Area and Volume**

Part 1. What did you learn?

SECTION 1

1. Polyhedrons are three-dimensional figures with polygon faces.

   A prism with n-gon polygons as bases has _____
   1
   faces, _____ vertices and _____
   2   3
   edges.

2. Visualize or make a 3-D drawing of a hexagonal prism. Determine how many faces, vertices and edges it has.

3. Explain how you know a prism with an n-gon base has $n + 2$ faces.

4.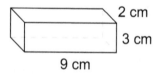
   2 cm
   3 cm
   9 cm

   a. Sketch the net of this prism. Label dimensions on the net.

   b. Make an orthogonal drawing of the prism.

5. Draw the top, front and right side views of the structure shown below. Discuss any problems that might come up if you used these orthogonal views to make a 3-D drawing.

   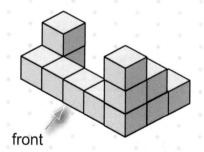
   front

6. A pyramid with an *n*-gon polygon as a base has (*n* + 1) faces, (*n* + 1) vertices, and 2*n* edges. Explain why each of these relationships makes sense. Use some of the words in the "Mathematically Speaking" boxes from Section 1 in your explanation.

SECTION 2

7. What is the sum of the measures of the angles of any triangle?

8. LuAnne practiced her guitar from 4:45 pm until 5:20 pm How many degrees did the minute hand on LuAnne's watch move during her practice time? Show or explain how you got your answer.

9. For each of the following, fill in *all, some* or *no* to make a true statement.

a. _____ reflex angles are less than 180°.

b. _____ triangles have two obtuse angles.

c. _____ triangles have three 60° angles.

d. _____ pairs of vertical angles are equal.

e. _____ pairs of angles that add up to 90° are supplementary.

f. Choose two of the statements above and justify your response.

10. ∠1 in the figure below measures 25° and ∠5 measures 74°. Find the measures of ∠2, ∠3, ∠4 and ∠6.

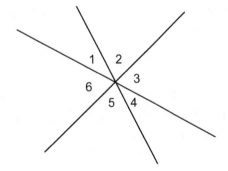

11. Your friend says that the volume of a shoe box is 1,008 cubic inches. What does this mean?

12. Describe three ways to find the surface area of the prism below.

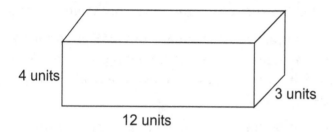

4 units

3 units

12 units

13. **a.** Fill in the blanks: The volume of a prism is the amount of material that _____ the prism. Volume is also
        1

defined as the amount of _____ the prism occupies.
                          2

b. Find the volume of the prism in Question 12 above. Show your work.

14. Fill in the blanks: Capacity is the _____ volume
                                            1

a container can hold. We measure capacity using units such

as _____, _____ and
      2   3

_____. Usually we use the term capacity when
    4

we are describing the amount of _____ a container
                                  5

would hold.

15. A fish tank in the shape of a rectangular prism is 80 centimeters long, 50 centimeters wide and 40 centimeters high. What is its capacity? Find the capacity in both mL and L.

16. Jaelyn is in charge of the props for the school play, Jack and the Beanstalk. She has to make a giant shoe box where the dimensions are all 4 times the original length. Discuss how the volume of Jaelyn's giant shoe box compares to the volume of the original shoe box.

17. David was asked the following question on a recent study quiz.

    The circumference of a pizza is 44 inches. What is the approximate area of the pizza? Use 3.14 for π.

    David said, "I can't answer this question because it does not include the radius of the pizza."

    What is wrong with David's reasoning? Explain.

18. Station WSBU can be heard in a circular area of approximately 20,000 square miles that is centered at its transmitter. What is the greatest distance you can live from the transmitter and still hear it? Use 3.14 as an approximation for π and round your answer to the nearest tenth.

19. Maya calculated the surface area of the triangular prism whose net is pictured below.

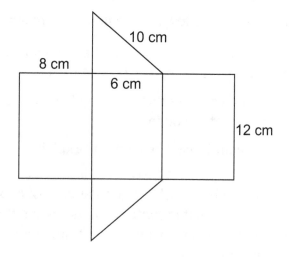

Here is her work and explanation:

Area of base: 0.5(6)(8) = 24 cm²

24 • 2 = 48 cm² (for both bases)

Lateral surface: 6 + 6 + 6 = 18 cm

18 • 12 = 216 cm²

Total surface area: 216 + 48 = 264 cm²

First, I found the area of each base by using the formula for the area of a triangle. Then, I doubled it. The lateral surface is a rectangle that is 18 by 12 so I found 18 • 12 to get 216. I added these answers to get the surface area.

Find and correct the error(s) in Maya's reasoning. What would you say to Maya to help her realize her mistake(s)?

20. Kim Lee was asked to find the volume of the skateboard ramp pictured below.

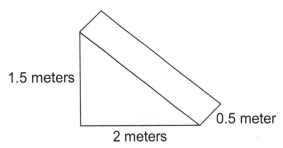

1.5 meters

0.5 meter

2 meters

Here is what he wrote:

$V = Bh$

The base of this ramp is a rectangle that is 2 • 0.5. So the area is 2 • 0.5 = 1 m².

The height is 1.5 meters. So, the volume is 1 • 1.5 = 1.5 m³.

Find and correct the error(s) in Kim Lee's reasoning. Calculate the actual volume of the ramp. What would you say to Kim Lee to help him realize his mistake(s)?

21. Leon was asked to find the area of the shape below.

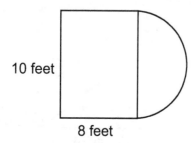

10 feet

8 feet

He said, "I don't think I can determine the area since we are not given the radius of the semicricle." What might you say to Leon to help him figure out how to use the given information to find the radius of the semicircle and the area of the figure?

22. On a recent quiz, Tamara was asked to find the measure of angle *CAB* in the triangle below. She said it is probably 45° since it "looks a little bigger than angle *ACB*." What would you say or do to help Tamara find the true measure of angle *CAB*?

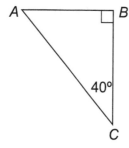

A   B

40°

C

Glossary

angle A figure formed by two rays that share a common endpoint, called the vertex.

Example:

apex The vertex opposite the base of a pyramid or cone.

Example:

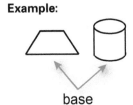

base The side of a two-dimensional figure or the face(s) of a three-dimensional shape recognized as the bottom of that figure or shape. A prism has two bases.

Example:

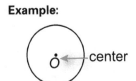

capacity The greatest volume a container can hold.

center (of a circle) The fixed point, O, from which all points on the circle are equidistant.

Example:

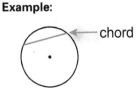

chord A line segment with its endpoints on the circle.

Example:

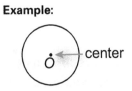

circle The set of all points that are the same distance from a fixed point called the center.

Example:

center

circumference The distance around the edge of a circle; equal to the product of the diameter of the circle and pi.

Example:

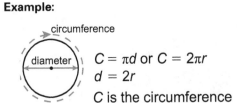

$C = \pi d$ or $C = 2\pi r$
$d = 2r$
C is the circumference

concentric (circles) Circles with the same center point.

Example:

cone A three-dimensional shape that has a single curved base and an apex. A circular cone has a circle as a base.

Example:

cone

cross section A two-dimensional region formed when a plane intersects a solid.

Example:

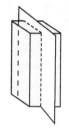

cube A three-dimensional shape with six square faces.

Example:

cube

cylinder A three-dimensional shape with two parallel circular bases.

Example:

cylinder

diameter The distance across a circle through its center. Also, the line segment through the center with endpoints on the circle.

Example:

$d = 2r$
d is the diameter

dimension The measures used to describe the size of a shape. The number of measures needed to describe a figure or shape geometrically.

Examples:

A 1-D line is described by one measure, or dimension its length.

A 2-D figure is described by two measures, or dimensions such as length and width or base and height.

A 3-D an object or space figure is described by three measures, or dimensions such as length, width, and height.

edge A line segment where two faces of a polyhedron meet.

Example:

edges

face A flat two-dimensional surface of a three-dimensional shape.

Example:

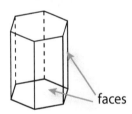

faces

goniometer A device used to measure an angle.

Example:

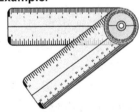

irrational number A real number that cannot be written in the form $\frac{a}{b}$, where a and b are integers and $b \neq 0$.

Example:

$\sqrt{2}$ and π

isometric drawing A drawing on isometric dot paper that shows a vertex and vertical edge of a shape in the foreground, and keeps the size and shape of an object the same.

Example:

lateral surface A face of a three-dimensional shape that is not considered a base.

Example:

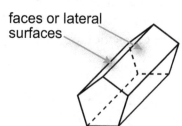

faces or lateral surfaces

---

lateral-surface rectangle The rectangle formed by the lateral surfaces of a prism, as seen in its net.

Example:

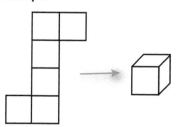

---

net A two-dimensional pattern that, when cut out and folded, makes a three-dimensional shape.

Example:

---

oblique prism A prism where the angles formed by the bases and the lateral faces are not right angles. Therefore, its lateral faces are non-rectangular parallelograms.

Example:

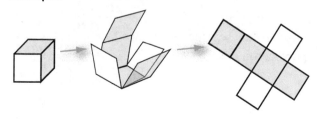

---

orthogonal drawing A drawing that shows different views of an shape by looking at it perpendicularly from the top, bottom, front, back, left or right.

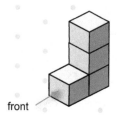

front

Example:

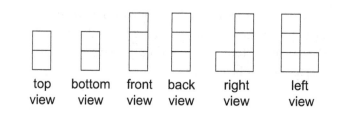

| top view | bottom view | front view | back view | right view | left view |

plane An undefined term in geometry. A flat surface that has no thickness, and extends forever in two dimensions.

perspective The technique of representing a three-dimensional object in two dimensions so that the object has the illusion of depth, and appears as one would normally see it.

pi The ratio of the circumference of a circle and its diameter. Pi is indicated by the symbol π. Pi is an irrational number that is approximately equal to 3.1416 or $\frac{22}{7}$.

polyhedron A three-dimensional shape that has polygons as faces. The plural of polyhedron is polyhedrons or polyhedra.

prism A three-dimensional shape with top and bottom faces that are congruent and parallel polygons (called "bases"). The other faces of a prism are called lateral surfaces. Prisms are named for the shape of their bases.

Example:

   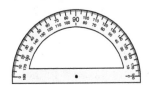

triangular prism   rectangular prism   square prism   pentagona prism

protractor A measuring device used to measure an angle.

Example:

pyramid A polyhedron with one base that is a polygon and triangles as the other faces (also called lateral surfaces). The triangles meet at the apex, the vertex opposite the base. Pyramids are named for the shape of their base.

Example:

square pyramid   triangular pyramid   hexagonal pyramid   pentagonal pyramid

radius The distance from the center of a circle to a point on the circle. Also, the line segment from the center of a circle to a point on the circle. The plural of radius is radii.

Example:

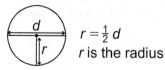

$r = \frac{1}{2}d$

r is the radius

reflex angle An angle whose measure is greater than 180 degrees, but less than 360 degrees.

Example:

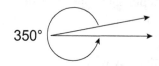

350°

right prism A prism where the angles formed by the bases and the lateral faces are right angles.

Example:

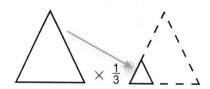

scale factor A number used as a multiplier to either enlarge or reduce the dimensions of an original object.

Example:

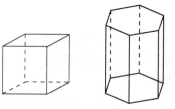

$\times \frac{1}{3}$

skew A description of two lines that do not lie in the same plane. Skew lines will never be parallel or intersect.

slant height The perpendicular length along the surface of a pyramid or cone from the apex to the base.

Example:

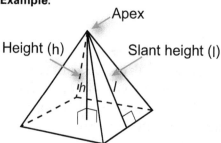

Apex

Height (h)

Slant height (l)

h

l

square (of a number) The product of a number and itself. The operation of squaring is indicated by a raised 2. For example, 3^2, read "3 squared" indicates the product 3 times 3.

Examples:

$3^2 = 3 \times 3 = 9$

$(0.4)^2 = 0.4 \times 0.4 = 0.16$

square number A number that equals the square of a whole number.

Examples:

16 is a square number since $4 \times 4 = 16$.

25 is a square number since $5 \times 5 = 25$.

square root A number that when multiplied by itself produces the given number.

Examples:

6 is the square root of 36 since $6 \times 6 = 36$.

0.5 is the square root of 0.25 since $0.5 \times 0.5 = 0.25$.

straight angle An angle with a measure of 180 degrees.

Example:

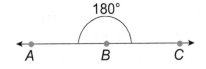

$m\angle ABC = 180°$

surface area The sum of the areas of all of the surfaces that make up a three-dimensional shape expressed in square units.

tetrahedron A triangular pyramid with identical equilateral triangles for all of its faces.

Example:

vertex A point where two or more edges of a shape meet. The plural of vertex is vertices.

Example:

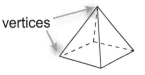

vertices

volume The amount of space contained in a three-dimensional solid expressed in cubic units.

Lesson 1.3

On Your Own

Page 25, Question 4: Congruent figures are exactly the same size and shape.

Lesson 3.3

On Your Own

Page 98, Question 4b: One way to estimate is to calculate a percentage of the total surface area.

Page 99, Question 7c: Remember: you cannot buy a fraction of a gallon of paint.

Lesson 3.6

On Your Own

Page 124, Question 4: Consider how many cubic centimeters are equivalent to 1 liter.

Index

E

edge (See also *bases, polyhedron*), 2, 4
  polyhedrons, 5, 9
  on prisms, 9
endpoint, common (See also *vertex*), 43, 52
Euclid, 41, 72
  Euclid's Elements, 41
Euler's Formula (See also *polyhedrons, prisms*), 10

F

faces (surfaces) (See also *bases, prisms, pyramids, three-dimensional shapes*), 2, 4, 5, 8
  bases connected by, 3
  cube, 3
  of polyhedrons, 2, 8, 34
  of prisms, 3, 26, 37
  of pyramids, 5
  square (of a rectangular prism), 3
formulas (See also *measure*)
  area, 87, 138
  Euler's Formula, 10
  number of faces in a prism, 37
  oblique prisms, 121, 122
  ratio between square and square root, 104
  rectangular prisms, 119–120
  surface area of prisms, 97, 113, 115
  volume, 119, 120, 123, 137
fractions
  squaring, 49

G

goniometer (See also *measure, protractor*), 53
graph (See also *Cartesian grid*)
  proportional relationship, 79

H

hexagonal prism (See also *prisms*), 4
hexagonal pyramid (See also *pyramid*), 5

I

intersect (See also *lines, parallel, skew lines*), 44, 48
irrational number (See also *circles, pi*), 80
isometric drawing (See also *drawing*), 23–24, 32, 33, 38
  dot paper, 23

L

lateral surface rectangle (See also *prisms*), 14, 15, 110
  folding along, 37
  formation of, 111
lateral surfaces (See also *prisms*)
  of prisms, 3, 14, 36
  of pyramids, 5
line(s) (See also *Euclid, line segment, parallel, plane, point, ray*), 42, 72
  intersecting, 44, 48
line segment (See also *line, point, ray*), 42–43, 72
  of polyhedron, 2
  radius defined as, 78

M

measure (See also *formulas*)
  angles using a protractor, 19, 53, 54
  area, 28, 86, 87, 91, 92, 119
  capacity, 122
  circumference (of a circle), 78
  degree, 50
  goniometer, 53
  oblique prisms, 121, 122
  protractor, 19, 53, 54
  ratio of circumference to diameter, 79
  solids, 13
  square units to, 40, 96
  surface area, 96, 102, 106, 110, 113, 115, 135
  trapezoid, 119
  triangle, area, 28, 95
  volume, 119, 123, 137
miniature (See *scale factor*)

T

tetrahedron (See *pyramids*)

three-dimensional shapes (See also *nets, polyhedrons, pyramids, prisms, shapes, spatial visualization*), 1

  bases, 3, 4, 8

  drawing, 21–22, 23–24, 28–30, 38

  edge, 2, 4

  faces (surfaces), 2, 4, 5, 8

  net as pattern for, 13, 16, 17

  pentominoes, 26

  polyhedrons, 1–2, 5, 36

  solids measured in, 13

  surface area of, 135

  volume of, 119, 120, 137

trapezoid (See also *shapes*), 119

  prism, 7

triangle (See also *shapes*), 62, 63

  angles of, 62, 68

  area, 28, 95

two-dimensional space (See also *nets, plane, three-dimensional shapes*), 6, 14, 26

  cross section, 37

  pentominoes, 26

V

vertex (pl. vertices) (See also *polyhedron*), 2, 4

  Euler's Formula, 10

  opposite base of pyramid (apex), 5

  positioning on a protractor, 53

vertical angles (See also *angles*), 60, 73

vertical distance (See also *prism*), 13

vertices (See *vertex*)

volume (See also *capacity, measure*), 119, 137

  cubic units to measure, 119

  formulas, 119, 120

  prism, 137

CPSIA information can be obtained
at www.ICGtesting.com
Printed in the USA
LVHW051100150721
692687LV00002B/4